"Kaiser and Little have done a big service to the evangelical community in setting forth a broad, biblical, and engaging presentation of the doctrine of creation. Their Biblical Portraits of Creation provides a refreshing picture covering important, but often neglected, biblical texts. Further, it contains some of the best material available on the historicity of the Genesis account of creation as opposed to contemporary critical and evolutionary denials. In addition, it captures the grandeur and majesty of the biblical text without stalling in the contemporary debate over the time of creation. It roots are deeply embedded in good biblical exposition and blossom in fruitful and bountiful portrayal of the most basic of all acts of our omnipotent God—the creation of the heavens and the earth!"

Norman L. Geisler, professor of apologetics,
Veritas Evangelical Seminary

"Christians of all confessions refer to the God of the Bible as the maker of heaven and earth. Biblical Portraits of Creation explores the dynamic doctrine of creation from Genesis through the Psalms and Prophets to Jesus himself. Combining scholarly depth and pastoral wisdom, Kaiser and Little have given us here a beautiful call to praise—a hallelujah book!"

Timothy George, dean, Beeson Divinity School
of Samford University

"The doctrine of creation holds crucial importance in the Christian theology of redemption. Kaiser and Little illustrate this point as they survey creation texts throughout the Historical, Wisdom, and Prophetic books of the Old Testament as well as in the Gospels and Epistles of the New Testament. Their integration of the creation message throughout the Bible's sixty-six books holds the key to resolving divisive contention over this topic among Christians. What's more, it brings renewed excitement to integrative study of the whole Word of God. I heartily recommend this book to all Christians. Its contents, notes, and study questions make it an excellent resource for pastors, teachers, and Bible study leaders.

Hugh Ross, astronomer, author, pastor,
and president of Reasons to Believe

"The sermons published in this important book will help Christians read key biblical passages with fresh eyes, think more biblically about creation, and appreciate with renewed gratefulness the wonder of the world."

Eckhard J. Schnabel, Mary F. Rockefeller Distinguished Professor
of New Testament, Gordon-Conwell Theological Seminary

WALTER KAISER JR. AND DORINGTON G. LITTLE

BIBLICAL PORTRAITS OF CREATION

CELEBRATING THE MAKER OF HEAVEN AND EARTH

WEAVER BOOK
COMPANY
WOOSTER, OHIO

Biblical Portraits of Creation: Celebrating the Maker of Heaven and Earth
© 2014 by Walter C. Kaiser Jr. and Dorington G. Little

Published by
Weaver Book Company
1190 Summerset Dr.
Wooster, OH 44691
weaverbookcompany.com

Cover design: StoryLook Design
Editorial, design, and production:
  { In a Word } www.inawordbooks.com
  /edited by Katherine Pickett/

Library of Congress Cataloging–in–Publication Data
Kaiser, Walter C.
  Biblical portraits of creation : celebrating the maker of heaven and earth / Walter C. Kaiser Jr. & Dorington G. Little.—1st [edition].
    pages cm
    Includes index.
    ISBN 978-0-9891671-1-6
  1. Creationism—Biblical teaching. 2. Creation—Biblical teaching.
  3. Bible—Commentaries. I. Title.
    BS680.C69K35 2014
    231.7'65—dc23
                        2014000588
Printed in the United States of America
14 15 16 17 18 / 5 4 3 2 1

With thanksgiving to our Lord
for the special gift of
our wives:

Elizabeth A. Little
&
In memoriam
Margaret Ruth Kaiser (1932–2013)

Contents

PREFACE

Walter C. Kaiser Jr.

*I*t is a pleasure for Dr. Dorington Little and me to present this book to each of you as lay readers and pastors alike. In the providence of God, I had prepared six of these chapters as sermons that were given at the Cannon Beach Christian Conference in Cannon Beach, Oregon, in the summer of 2013. About this same time, my wife, Marge, who would shortly after this go to be with the Lord, urged me to listen with her to Dori's Sunday sermon on her iPod, which turned out to be a sermon based on Psalm 148. Previously, while we had lived and worked in New England, Marge and I had been blessed to be part of his church at the First Congregational Church of Hamilton (MA). But now that we had retired to Wisconsin, we had missed his sermons and the fellowship of the church immensely. But Marge was a faithful listener of Pastor Little's exposition of the Word of God.

As I listened to Dori's exposition of Psalm 148, it seemed as if I were being prompted by the Lord to call Dori on the phone and ask if he would like to join me as a contributor and as a coauthor in the project I had been working on called *Biblical Portraits of Creation*. His positive response set the stage for his contribution on Psalm 148 plus two more chapters, which are on Matthew 1:1–17 and 2 Corinthians 4:6 and 5:17, as well as many important revisions and additions to some of what I had already written.

So the result of our collaboration is by God's providence now in your hands. May each of you find the same joy we have found in bringing this material together for the honor and glory of our Lord.

To make this volume even more useful, a series of study questions and points for discussion have been added at the end of each chapter. Bible study is always much more valuable when it is done with others. So why not form a small group and meet weekly in a home or a convenient spot and then share the answers to the study questions? Do one lesson each week. By so doing you will encourage each other and begin to experience the community and love of the body of Christ. Let us know what some of your experiences are as you enjoy God's Word in such a growth group. God bless you, each one.

THE HEAVENS ARE TELLING THE GLORY OF GOD

Walter C. Kaiser Jr.

*T*he account of creation in the Bible is one of today's hottest topics. Unfortunately, the heated debate is too often carried on by evangelical scholars in seminars, either behind closed doors or in open forums of invective against fellow believers. What has raised this topic to the top of the list of issues for discussion is the outstanding success of the Human Genome Project, led by the evangelical Francis Collins in the 1990s. Ever since he and his team completed mapping out every gene in the human body (an amazing achievement by any standard), as was announced in 2001, under his leadership, the implications of this research for a biblical view of creation have loomed large in the thinking of many leaders in the community of faith. Added to this pressure has been the appearance of a new blog called "BioLogos," in which many evangelical scientists and theologians are involved. The effect of these two happenings has been a somewhat gentle disaffection from the view that God directly created the universe in favor of the revival of an old view, called theistic evolution, now, however, with some new twists.

It is not as if the scientific biological facts have all been in favor of one side or the other, but many evangelical theologians and exegetes are worried that once again the church will be caught off guard defending a view of origins just as it happened centuries ago when the church of that day argued that the earth stood still and was the center of the universe, instead of a heliocentric view of the universe, to the discomfort of Galileo. That, of course, proved to be disastrously incorrect. It is now being assumed that once again exegetes of Scripture will be caught off guard as they too defend what many now regard to be a view of creation that will not be sustainable in light of the facts discovered from genetic research.

However, compounding the problem is the fact that there has been a serious hiatus in the preaching mission of the church on the texts of Scripture that deal with creation. The negligence of the Church for including in its preaching mission interpretations and the application of some, or all, of the numerous biblical texts that deal with the Bible's claims for God's involvement in creation has often left the believing laity vulnerable to teaching that has often just plain vacated the topic of creation, or on the other hand has cast itself in violent reaction to any of the legitimate gains that science has made. Therefore, as a contribution to this much-needed topic, this volume on creation is set forth as an antidote for this hiatus.

This set of chapters contains teaching guides or preaching outlines that will serve as a stimulus to help God's people—and, hopefully, many spiritual shepherds—to get up to speed on how the Bible presents the topic of creation in all of its variations and what responses are called for by the believing community. After all, many of us recite each Lord's Day that we believe in "God the Father, Maker of heaven and earth!" What do we mean when we openly declare before God that this is our conviction?

Not only has the topic of creation been sadly neglected in our teaching and preaching ministries, but so has the whole corpus of Scripture been neglected, for there is a virtual famine of hearing and doing the Word of God in the land today (Amos 8:11). For example, in surveys taken by various pollsters, when asked in a multiple-choice question who gave the Sermon on the Mount, an overwhelming majority of respondents say Billy Graham instead of Jesus!

For some, this paucity of information in responding to the powerful Word of God may well be traced back to Marcion's attack on the Old Testament and the God of the Old Testament around AD 130, for he thought both the Old Testament and the God of the Old Testament were sub-Christian. Even though the church rejected these outrageous insinuations against the Old Testament and against God himself, nevertheless, a quiet emphasis began to build among the believing community that focused on the personal plan of salvation. Simultaneously, this shift quietly dropped any Christian thinking in terms of a personal Creator, the world, and creation itself, thereby handicapping our understanding of the new creation in Christ as well. Instead, the focus of biblical scholars fell on the exodus from Egypt as being the central motif of Scripture, while the idea of creation and God's work in nature and his coming kingdom and the new heavens and the new earth were reduced to a secondary, or even to a lesser level, or else simply abandoned altogether. This, in turn, has produced a type of dualistic mentality in which the physical world is set in opposition to the spiritual world. Out of this fray, appearing as early as the middle of the second Christian century, came the church's early battle with Gnosticism. But even though the church generally won that battle, a residual aspect of this dualistic thinking has continued to haunt the church to this day. Nevertheless, the God of creation and the God of redemption are the same God we worship and find in Scripture.

Meanwhile, the church did continue to assert the ancient formulas of the creeds that said, "I believe in God the Father Almighty, Maker of heaven and earth." Christian believers today have repeated, often unthinkingly, the Apostle's Creed in church services, which harkens back to at least the fourth Christian century, a form that also was part of the Nicene Creed. So why do some believers now express such doubt and uncertainties over the identity of the one who made the earth, and all that is in it, or who was directly responsible for the entire universe by speaking it into existence by the word of his mouth? Why is there such strong and hostile antagonism and disputes recently over even the word *creation* itself among evangelical believers, and about who owns that word *creation*, whether the young earth group of creation-science, the old earth contingent of believers, or the theistic creation evolutionists? In fact, the polarization and entrenchment along party lines grows more divisive and acrimonious each day. This is happening even though a large number of believers continue to repeat each Lord's Day these same venerable lines of the Apostles' and Nicene Creeds, especially in many of our mainline churches, yet without any teaching that would further explain what we mean or intend to assert by this affirmation!

Historically, anyone who acknowledged that God made the universe and created the life on it was called a creationist. That meaning is still a valid use of the word. However, in the past several decades, a new meaning has emerged: for some, the term *creationist* is reserved for those who believe in a *recent* creation, or in *creation-science,* which requires treating the six days of creation in Genesis as six consecutive, literal twenty-four-hour periods of time, in which God created all things, with a date for creation somewhere around 6,000 to 10,000 years before the present day. This group has also become known as the young earth group. They, too, are part of the body of Christ, of course, but their insistence on an earth of recent vintage, and a creation within the time span of one week, has unfortunately signaled a family feud that forces some to separate in their fellowship with believers of a different conclusion on these same matters, rather than a vigorous discussion with fellow believers, who are part of the body of Christ and who do affirm a view of origins that has God as the one who made all things by his speaking them into existence by the word of his mouth.

In the past two decades, another group of persons dealing with the issue of creation has emerged. Known as the Intelligent Design Movement (IDM), the group advocates that the real purpose and plan to all of life as we experience it today was created by an intelligent designer. This concept also has had a long history, for many in the past century or two have read William Paley's nineteenth-century *Natural Theology* (1802), in which Paley argues that there is so much design and purpose in the world of nature and its living organisms that it demands a maker who exhibits the intelligence and design abilities seen behind all the parts that make up this world. However, this IDM group, in its contemporary forms, generally declined to announce what this designer or maker's name might be. They hoped that this would remove all religious biases associated with their view and thus it would be allowed in America's public school classrooms as a neutral contribution to the discussion of origins. But this move was unacceptable to the American courts, just as it was for those who espoused creation-science, or the young earth view.

For Americans, the issue of creation versus evolution first went to the public forum of the courtroom in 1925, in the famous Scopes trial. The battle in this case was whether a teacher could teach evolution in American public schools. Advocates for creationism strenuously fought to prevent this view from entering public school classes in America. Evolutionists, however, decried this as a limitation on their freedom of speech.

Four additional court cases followed the 1925 Scopes trial: *Epperson v. Arkansas* (1968), *McLean v. Arkansas* (1981), *Aguillard v. Treen* (1983), and *Edwards v. Aguillard* (1987). In each of these four cases, the teaching of creation was pitted specifically against the First Amendment's establishment clause, which says:

> Congress shall make no law respecting an establishment of religion,
> or prohibiting the free exercise thereof; or abridging the freedom
> of speech, or of the press; or the right of the people peacefully to
> assemble, and to petition the Government for a redress of grievances.

But if any harmony was to come among the people of God on the topic of creation, it would have to come, first of all, through a return to the teaching and solid exposition of Scripture in our churches, and then an accompanying careful study of all the scientific evidence in all its detail in our schools and institutions of higher learning.

What has complicated the profitable joining of this debate in the twentieth and now into the twenty-first century, is the hiatus or the absence of the general teaching on what the Scriptures have to offer on this subject. To reverse this severe problem in the body of Christ, Rev. Dr. Dorington Little and I have projected in this volume a series of expositions of selected texts that focus on the teaching of creation from the Scripture, ranging from the topic of origins to our new creation in Christ and ending in the new heavens and the new earth. If all sides in this debate are to be heard, it would seem reasonable to allow the actual teaching of Scripture to have the place of honor at the table, just as an offer should be made to all of the other contributors who work in science as well.

But the introduction of the teaching blocks of Scripture is not all that simple, for the issue of how to interpret these passages immediately emerges as the elephant in the room. Take, for example, the magnificent description of creation in Genesis 1. Should that piece be understood as pure poetry, a poem, or was it cast in the genre of a myth, an allegory, or was it meant to be a historical prose narrative? The answers to these hermeneutical questions will result in a wide difference in interpretation. Therein lies one of the reasons for a world of such wide difference in how to treat the biblical statements on creation, for each answer will lead to a different conclusion and reading of the text. But this must not discourage us, for this problem too is soluble.

In 1968 I wrote an article for the twentieth anniversary of the Evangelical Theological Society (ETS) titled "The Literary Form of Genesis 1–11,"[1] which is included in the Appendix. To be sure, there has been

---

[1] Walter C. Kaiser Jr., "The Literary Form of Genesis 1–11," in *New Perspectives on the Old Testament,* ed. J. Barton Payne (Waco, TX: Word, 1970), 48–65. The article has long since been out of print.

a lot of change in the meantime, but then again, much has remained the same as to the heart of the issues themselves. Among the numerous challenges that various scholars have posed for understanding these chapters has been the issue of the literary form (or in German, its *Gattung*) of Genesis 1–11, which was taken up in that 1968 article as well. But a battery of labels suggested for these chapters by various scholars seemed to fail, as some suggested *parable*, others *myth*, and still others *poetry*. Our conclusion was that there was every indication that the original writer meant these chapters to be understood as narrative prose, rather than as parable, myth, poetry, or even as borrowings from the ancient Near Eastern cosmological stories about the doings of the gods and goddesses of that ancient Near Eastern era.

Primary evidence for this bold assertion could be found first of all in the recurring heading given to this material in Genesis 1–11: "These are the generations/histories of," an organizing rubric that appears strategically six times (Gen. 2:4; 5:1; 6:9; 10:1; 11:10, 27). This form easily links Genesis 1–11 with the patriarchal narrative in Genesis 12–50, which uses the identical heading five more times (Gen. 25:12, 19; 36:1, 9; 37:2). This would indicate that the writer meant for his material in Genesis 1–11 to be treated the same way as the material in Genesis 12–50. These later patriarchal chapters were found to contain much more background material from archaeological writings that gave the selections a note of authenticity.

Nevertheless, the protests continued as some still tried to build a case for a poetic characteristic in these chapters of 1–11. But the prevalent and repeated contact with hard reality could still be seen in some sixty-four geographical terms, another eighty-eight personal names, forty-eight generic names, and at least twenty-one identifiable cultural items such as gold, bdellium, onyx, brass, iron, gopher wood, bitumen, mortar, brick, stone, harp, pipe, cities, a tower, and more. To get an idea of a contrast, note that the single chapter of Genesis 10 has five times more geographical detail than the entire book of Koran. The point is this: every single detail in the Scripture presents the possibility of either establishing the reliability of the biblical writer or proving its falsehood, for each of these geographical, personal names or cultural elements make the text vulnerable to falsification if they do not appear when and as they are claimed to exist!

This does not mean that there are no figures of speech or any figurative language in Genesis 1–11. In fact, E. W. Bullinger listed some 150 different illustrations of figures of speech in Genesis 1–11.[2] But the controls on interpreting these forms were not arbitrary. Rather, they could be conducted by accurately supplying the name of the trope from classical sources, supplying a definition of the figure of speech, and illustrating it both from biblical and classical sources.

But the occasional use of a figurative expression does not determine the whole literary form. Nor are we left to our own devices to determine what is or is not poetry or prose, parable or allegory. In the case of Genesis 1–11, it is surprisingly simple to determine that this is not poetry, but prose. The use of the Hebrew *waw* consecutive verbs to describe sequential acts, the frequent use of the direct object sign, the use of the so-called relative pronoun (few, if any, occur in Hebrew poetry), the stress of definitions, and the spreading out of the events in a sequential order—all of these are sure Hebrew indications that we are dealing with prose and not poetry. Say what we will, the author of Genesis 1–2 wanted his work to be viewed as a narrative-prose form, just as he wanted his narratives about Abraham, Isaac, and Jacob to be understood in like manner.

All of this brings us to the acknowledged "Continental Divide" in biblical scholarship. The University of Chicago's Langdon B. Gilkey wrote what must be regarded as one of the greatest religious articles in the twentieth century (which I for one am willing to affirm as being one of the greatest in the twentieth century). He confessed that his own stance on biblical matters and that of most modern liberal biblical scholars of his ilk were "half liberal and modern on the one hand, and half Biblical and orthodox on the other, i.e., its world view or cosmology [wa]s modern while its theological language [wa]s biblical and orthodox." He went on to explain:

> What has happened is clear: because of our modern cosmology, we have stripped what we regard as "the biblical point of view" of all its wonders and voices. . . . [W]e have rejected as invalid all the innumerable cases of God's acting and speaking.[3]

---

[2] E. W. Bullinger, *Figures of Speech Used in the Bible* (1898; repr., Grand Rapids: Baker, 1968), 1032–33.

[3] Langdon B. Gilkey, "Cosmology, Ontology, and the Travail of Biblical Language," *Concordia Theological Monthly* 33 (1965): 152. This article is reprinted from *Journal of Religion* (1961): 194–205.

That analysis of the situation could not be more accurately stated. If progress is to be found in this discussion between science and biblical interpretation, priority must be given to the biblical writers' truth assertions and intentions and what they meant by their use of the words that they spoke on behalf of the God of heaven.

So we commend these chapters on Psalms, Job, Proverbs, Genesis, Isaiah, and the New Testament examples of Matthew and 2 Corinthians to each of you as probes to stimulate a whole new conversation on the Bible's extensive view on creation. And may these stimuli be used among laypersons, as well as among our pastors and teachers of the Word of God, to interact with the new findings of science. God is the source of everything that is true, so do not fear a possible intimidation from some unsuspected new findings from science that will blow a big hole in the case for "I believe in God the Father, Maker of heaven and earth!"

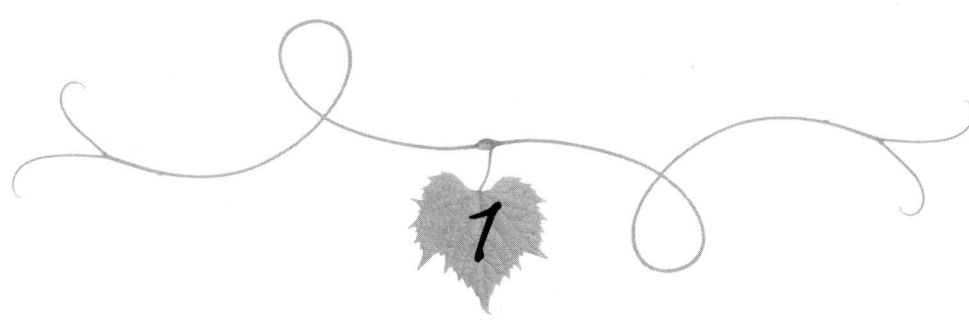

WISDOM WAS THERE BEFORE GOD CREATED THE WORLD

PROVERBS 3:19–20; 8:22–31

Walter C. Kaiser Jr.

*I*n Proverbs 8, wisdom is not represented as a deity similar to Egypt's *ma`at*. Instead, wisdom is represented as a personification of one of God's attributes, one that was instrumental in his work of creating the world. Many in the history of interpretation have equated wisdom directly with Jesus Christ, but wisdom is only a personification of one of the divine qualities. The apostle Paul described the fulfillment of wisdom in Christ (Col. 1:15–20; 2:3), but wisdom was never raised to a separate person in the Godhead, as in a hypostatic union with Christ, nor was wisdom ever treated as if it were only another name for the second person of the Trinity. So it would be incorrect to view wisdom as the preincarnate person of Christ in Proverbs 8.

However, the supposition that wisdom, as it is depicted in Proverbs 8:22–31, is one of the key attributes that was present with our Lord as he created the world, can be seen first of all in Proverbs 3:19–20. In that text, not only is wisdom described as a quality in God's being, by which he created the world, but alongside the use of his wisdom is his understanding and his knowledge. These three gifts were used by God as he "marked out the foundations of the earth," "set the heavens in place," and "fixed securely the fountains of the deep" (8:27–29).[1] Certainly, this pointed to the fact that God alone was the sole initiator and the one forming all of

---

[1] All Scripture quotations for my chapters, unless otherwise indicated, are from the NIV.

this cosmos. Priority of place, however, was given to God's wisdom, for it came first in the order of things.

Proverbs 8:22–31 builds on the foundational statement already mentioned in Proverbs 3:19–20. But it takes the narrative of the creation of the world all the way back to the beginning, as 8:22–23 provides a summary of the fact that the Lord possessed wisdom even before the creation of the world. Then, in 8:24–31, the summary statement of the opening verses of Proverbs 3:19–20 is developed, as the passage gives a lengthier account as to how wisdom functioned as an agent of creation in the divine handiwork.

Focal Point:	v. 22 "The Lord brought me forth as the first of his works, before his deeds of old."
Homiletical Keyword:	Actions
Interrogative:	What? (What were the actions God took in using Wisdom as he created the world?)

I.   Wisdom Came as the First of God's Works (Prov. 8:22–23)

II. Wisdom Was Established before the Creation of the World (Prov. 8:24–26)

III. Wisdom Witnessed Two of the Lord's Most Impressive Creative Acts (Prov. 8:27–29)

IV. Wisdom Rejoiced in All of Creation, Especially Humanity (Prov. 8:30–31)

I.   Wisdom Came as the First of God's Works (Prov. 8:22–23)

The meaning of "brought me forth" has been a warmly contested line ever since the controversy with Arius's followers in the early church. Arius (ca. AD 250–336), who was of Libyan descent, was excommunicated because he used just such a clause as this one to declare that the Son of God was essentially inferior to the Father and was the first of God's creations, as this wisdom text shows. This reduced God the Son to one who did not have eternal existence but one who had been born after God the Father.

The Hebrew word used here is *qanah,* which can mean "to create," but most interpreters argue that in this context it means not "to create" but "to become a parent of," "to procreate." Therefore, if we understand this metaphor to mean "to become a parent of," wisdom had to come from God's essential being as part of his attributes. Wisdom has an organic connection with the very nature of God and his being.

Since wisdom existed before creation, it is distinct from creation and is accessible to humanity by the gift of revelation. But what is certainly denied here is that Yahweh had a sexual partner in the begetting of wisdom. Rather, wisdom came from God's very being. All literal interpretations of this metaphor will lead only to a polytheistic rendering of this concept; understanding it as a metaphor makes better sense.

This procreation of wisdom was the first (Hebrew *re'shit*) in the time of God's acts of working. Thus, God's begetting of wisdom was the earliest of his deeds, even before God's ancient deeds of making the universe (v. 22b). Notice how in John's Gospel (1:1–3; cf. Col. 1:15–16), the Word (*logos*) was similarly world-creating in his work. This work God reviewed in Genesis 1:4, 9, 12, and elsewhere, and he pronounced all of it "very good."

Wisdom was "appointed" (or "fashioned," "formed," Hebrew *nissakti*) way back in eternity (v. 23). All of this was "when the world came to be" (v. 23b). In this way wisdom could be present during the work of creation and witness all that God would do.

II. WISDOM WAS ESTABLISHED BEFORE THE CREATION OF THE WORLD (PROV. 8:24–26)

The second strophe wants to stress the fact that wisdom had its beginning long before the world began. Five time markers are given in verses 24–26 to show that wisdom preexisted the cosmos. The first time marker is "when there were no oceans" (v. 24a). Regarding the word "oceans" (or "depths," Hebrew *tehomot*), some try to connect it with the primeval abyss, but the reference to springs in the parallel line of verse 24b suggests that "oceans" is intended here. It is important to notice that there is no reference to God contending with a chaos monster of the sea, as is found in ancient Near Eastern myths of origins.

The second time marker is found in verse 24b: "there were no springs abounding with water." In much of the parched land of the Near East, nothing was more important to the sustaining of life as were those places where water springs up from the subterranean depths to water the earth, the animals, and humans. But Wisdom preceded the appearance of all of these springs.

Wisdom also predated the time when "mountains were settled in place" (v. 25a). The mountains are depicted as having their roots in the depths of the sea as they rise out of the waters (Ps. 104:6–8). Some regard the mountains as the oldest parts of the earth (cf. Ps. 90:1–2; Micah 6:2), but wisdom was ahead of them. The same claim could be made about the hills (v. 25b), for preceding them, wisdom "was given birth." But what must not be missed is that wisdom was being used to create the world with its oceans, springs, mountains, and hills. The work of creation itself, however, was the work of God.

In verse 26 we come to the fifth time marker, but all of a sudden we are introduced to a "he," who is the real agent of creation—he who made the earth and its fields. The word "made" is one of the common words (Hebrew *'asah*) used in Genesis that refers to the Lord's creative activity. Even more exciting is the fact that God made "the dust of the earth" (v. 26b). Could this text be referring to Adam, who was made from the "dust of the ground" (Gen. 2:7)? Surely, Adam was made from the "dust," but did this text allude to that event also?

Wisdom, no matter which way the form of expression is taken, claims to be older than the dust of the world. If this is indeed a veiled reference to the formation of Adam from dust, then this allusion to man coming from the dirt surely indicates once again the fragility and mortality of mortals. Wisdom was first to appear in this world before men and women arrived.

III. Wisdom Witnessed Two of the Lord's Most Impressive Creative Acts (Prov. 8:27–29)

Wisdom claims to have been present at two of the most spectacular events in creation: the making of the heavens and the placing of restraints on the power and extent of the seas. This indicates, at the very least, that the universe was made of the principles of wisdom. How foolish it would be for anyone to live contrary to the principles of wisdom.

Because wisdom was present at creation, she had an opportunity to contemplate and celebrate the way God decreed it and brought it all about. Not only did our Lord "set the heavens in place," but he "marked out the horizon on the face of the deep" (v. 27b). Some have rendered the word "horizon" incorrectly as the "vault [of the heavens]," but that concept comes from Near Eastern mythology rather than from the Hebrew text itself.

God also "established" (or "made firm") the "clouds above" (v. 28a), just as he also provided the ample water supply in the "fountains of the deep" (v. 28b). Moreover, God "gave the sea its boundary so the waters would not overstep his command" (v. 29). Thus, God put limits on the sea so that it would not flood out the mortals he had made. The sea would be restrained for the good of the earth (cf. Job 38:10; Ps. 148:6; Jer. 5:22; Ps. 93; 104:6–9).

IV. Wisdom Rejoiced in All of Creation, Especially Humanity (Prov. 8:30–31)

Verse 30 of Proverbs 8 forms an inclusion with verse 27: "I was there" and "I was constantly at his side." Wisdom says, according to the Hebrew text, that she was "the craftsman" (Hebrew 'amon), but how shall we render this word? When God's work is rendered as involving wisdom as a craftsman, it diffuses the message that the Lord was the creator of all things. So how could wisdom be called an artisan or a craftsman? It is best to render as a Hebrew Qal infinitive absolute meaning "to be firm," "faithful." Therefore, a more accurate rendering is "and I was beside him *faithfully;* and I was delighting daily in celebrating before him at all times" (v. 30, emphasis mine). Wisdom was delighting in God's handiwork in creation "day after day" (or "daily"), which implies that creation took place over a period of time. In fact, wisdom did not stop celebrating the fact that God had created it all.

But what wisdom especially rejoiced in was the creation of "mankind" (v. 31b). No reference is made to the image of God in mortals as being a reason for such celebratory joy, but something like this must have provoked wisdom's delight and joy.

CONCLUSIONS

1. Before God made the world, he brought forth wisdom as if it were one who would be alongside him to witness all his work.
2. God is described as the maker of heaven and earth in all of its provisions.
3. Wisdom rejoiced especially in the creation of man and woman.

STUDY QUESTIONS AND DISCUSSION STARTERS

1. How does wisdom function in these texts? Is wisdom just another name for the second person of the Trinity, a personification of an attribute of God, or was it a literary convention of that day?
2. How did the Arian heresy misuse the expression in Proverbs 8:22, "brought me forth"? What is the correct understanding of the phrase?
3. What were the five markers given in Proverbs 8:24–26 to show that wisdom preexisted the origin of the cosmos?
4. What, according to this text, were two of the most spectacular events in creation at which wisdom was declared to be present? What significance is attached to wisdom's presence at that time (Prov. 8:27–29)?
5. How does Proverbs 8:30–31 represent the part that wisdom played in the creation events?
6. In what part of the creative order did wisdom find her highest celebratory joy? Discuss why you think this is true.

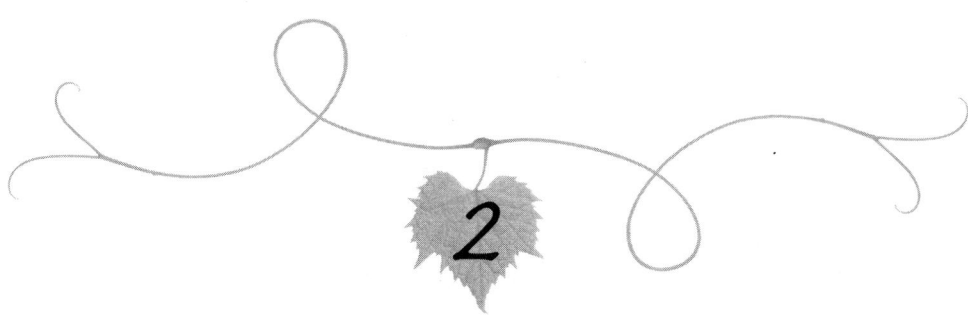

In the Beginning God Created the Universe

Genesis 1

Walter C. Kaiser Jr.

The Holy Scripture began its revelation to humanity with the narrative of the creation of all things in Genesis 1. Even though this text has been variously treated over the years of human study as being either a form of poetry, myth, creation-science, or some other type of literary form, our attempt will be to take it straightforwardly as its writer indicated that he meant it to be understood, based on the semantic or contextual signals given in the text. Only in this way can we begin to capture the thrill, joy, and majesty of what God has made in his creating the universe.

But here is the place to begin, for without a cosmos and an earth, there was no story, or anything to talk about, much less to live for. The divine act of creation is what started the whole narrative of the continuing plan of God and the purpose for which everything had been made. So, it is with this in mind that we turn to this majestic text that has occupied so much attention in so many of its details that the main idea has often almost been lost in the shuffle of modern life!

Focal Point:	v. 31 "God saw everything he had made, and it was very good."
Homiletical Keyword:	Actions

Interrogative: What?
                                  (What were the actions God
                                  took in making this "very
                                  good" world that likewise
                                  calls for our rejoicing in all
                                  that God made?)

I.   OUR LORD CREATED MATTER, SPACE, AND TIME (GEN. 1:1–10)

II.   OUR LORD CREATED ALL PLANT LIFE (GEN. 1:11–13)

III. OUR LORD CREATED THE SUN, MOON, AND STARS (GEN. 1:14–19)

IV.   OUR LORD CREATED ALL ANIMAL LIFE (GEN. 1:20–25)

V.   OUR LORD CREATED ALL HUMAN LIFE (GEN. 1:26–31)

I.   OUR LORD CREATED MATTER, SPACE, AND TIME (GEN. 1:1–10)

The verdict expressed in verse 31 of Genesis 1 did not have reference merely to the divine work observed on the sixth workday of creation, but to the *entirety* of God's creation. In its entirety, God pronounced it all as being "very good," meaning it was pleasing and pleasant to our Maker as it should be to all of us as observers of the results of his handiwork. Six times previously (1:3, 10, 12, 18, 21, 24) God had pronounced his work "good," but now in review of it in its entirety, he pronounced all of his creative work "very good" (v. 31). This is the starting point from which the whole story of redemption and triumph must begin.

Surely this signaled God's delight, his approval, and his overall satisfaction with the work of his hands! Not only did his creation bring him pleasure, but there was nothing that had come from his hand that was not excellent and an exhibit of perfection! How could a good God do any less than that which was excellent in all its aspects? What he made was good—indeed "very good."

But we know that things did not remain that way, for a catastrophe enters this "very good" world by the time we get to the garden of Eden in Genesis 3. But that is not at all how these things began, for what is now spoiled and marred had not been made that way originally; it had been made "very good." However, even though sin had intruded its wicked head into our world in Genesis 3, men and women fell from a great height, for God had originally created it all in "very good" condition. That is what must be understood first of all.

In the first verse of Genesis 1, we are told, "God created the heavens and the earth." Before there was anything in God's "very good" work of creation, there was only God. He alone is and remains eternal! Therefore, he was in the beginning, for it was an absolute beginning of all that was to come among the things we see. Some have wanted to translate the opening words of the Bible somewhat like this: "*When* God began to create . . . *then* he said" (1:1–3).[1] The advantage of using this dependent clause translation for verses 1–2 is that it parallels the opening line of the Babylonian creation story entitled *Enuma Elish:* "When above, the heavens had not been named [and] below. . . ."

But there are strong reasons for opting for the Hebrew version as possessing an independent clause, rather than a dependent clause similar to the Babylonian story in Genesis 1:1. First, all the ancient versions translate the word as an absolute clause, "in the beginning."

Second, the Hebrew Masoretes, of the fifth or sixth Christian century, accented the word as an absolute, for they put a disjunctive mark, called a *tiphah,* rather than a conjunctive accent on the one Hebrew word translated as "in the beginning," thereby showing they treated it as an absolute beginning.

And third, there is an exact parallel usage in Isaiah 46:10, where the word "beginning" is also used in an absolute sense. So the meaning is, "in the beginning [implying the use of the article], God created the heavens and the earth." There was nothing prior to God or prior to his decision to act as the maker of heaven and earth. This was an absolute beginning with nothing preceding it except the person of God himself! Not even matter preexisted any of God's work in creation!

Since Hebrew has no word like our English word "universe," these two terms ("heaven" and "earth") form a figure of speech known as hendiadys, in which one concept or idea is expressed by two words. But the meaning is clear: God created everything, whether it was terrestrial or celestial!

---

[1] Recent translations include New English Bible, New American Bible, New Jerusalem Bible, Revised Standard Version, and Amplified Bible.

That includes matter, space, and time itself. All the raw material out of which God is going to fashion the universe is now on hand in verses 1–2.

But notice verse 2: "Now the earth was formless and empty, darkness was over the surface of the deep, and the Spirit of God was hovering over the waters." This seems to be the condition of the earth in its formative stages, for very few would call this "very good" (neither did God nor Genesis!). What can this mean except that there was emptiness, darkness, and desert-like conditions as the first evidence of the work of God on the planet began appearing. It was more like a vacant place, for at that point it was uninhabited. How could this be called a "good" or a "very good" work of God while it was still under construction?

A hint as to what may have happened here can be seen in a celestial disturbance that came somewhere in the universe, presumably even before the fall of Adam and Eve. This would have been the expulsion of Satan out of heaven, along with other angelic beings (Jude 6; 2 Peter 2:4). It must also be noticed that Lucifer, here named in Genesis 3 in Hebrew *hannahash,* "the serpent," later appears in the book of Revelation under the names of "the dragon," "the serpent," and "the devil" (Rev. 12:9). Thus, his fall into sin had to have preceded the fall of the human pair in the garden of Eden, for the serpent now represents evil and seems to have had access to the courts of heaven to know what might or might not happen to this hapless couple.

Thus, the Hebrew narrative had stopped in verse 2 long enough to record what had been happening in the mammoth task of shaping and building the universe (for beginning in verse 3, the Hebrew verbs use the narrative *wayyiqqtol* form, while in verse 2 the text is still confined to the perfect form of the Hebrew verb). But since the work had only started, it was not time to show how it all came together as yet. God would take what appeared at the moment to be more like what seemed to be unstructured and amorphous material and mold it and make it into a wonderful cosmos in the six steps that would follow beginning in verse 3.

Thus, the next action step in the organized work of God's creation was the creation of light (v. 3). God gave his fiat, merely by speaking the event into being, and, behold, there was light. He directly spoke light into its very existence, which would be his method of work in creation from here on out. In fact, nine times over (vv. 3, 6, 9, 11, 14, 20, 24, 26, and 29) in this first chapter, the text boldly announces: "And God said" in a narrative-prose form that traces the progress and method of creation.

The power and the theology of God's spoken word are often missed, but when we again meet God's spoken word in the New Testament, a centurion who meets Jesus in Matthew 8:5–13 requests that Jesus heal his servant. But he asks for our Lord merely to pronounce his word of healing without going to all the trouble of visiting the centurion's home, for if he speaks the word, the centurion is certain his servant will be healed. That is exactly what happens. No wonder John's Gospel takes the similar bold stance of declaring:

> In the beginning was the Word, and the Word was with God, and the Word was God. He was with God in the beginning. Through him all things were made; without him nothing was made that has been made. (John 1:1–3)

Surely this text points to the dual fact that creation came about by the spoken word of Jesus and that our Lord Jesus, in particular, also had a direct hand in all that currently appears on earth and in heaven.

It is interesting that light was necessary to begin the shaping process and for forming the cosmos wherein the man and the woman would live. That is why the darkness of verse 2, though not a separate force or entity apart from God's directive hand, was over the surface of the deep. God had to create darkness as well!

This was followed by God's creation of the firmament, or as it is better stated, a great expanse. This Hebrew term should not be rendered as a vault or a hard dome or canopy that encircled the sky above the earth, for those ideas came from the Greek (*stereoma*) and Latin (*firmamentum*) terms for this Hebrew word "expanse." It is best to view that expanse as the sky, the heavens, and the atmosphere.

This was followed by a third major creative action by God. He separated the dry land from the waters that were also present, so that great landmasses began to appear as the continents. These areas would be where the descendants of Adam and Eve would live.

II.   Our Lord Created All Plant Life (Gen. 1:11–13)

In the third act of God's creation, God empowered the earth to be his agent for his generative power, for it reads: "Then God said, 'Let the land produce vegetation: seed-bearing plants and trees on the land that bear fruit with seed in it'" (v. 11). And that is what happened: "The land produced vegetation" (v. 12). Previously, as a preparation for this event, God had ordered the dry land should appear (v. 9). But as the land appeared, God also made provision for the sustaining of his creation by placing the seeds in the plants and trees so that their preservation was also cared for.

But look at the variety and diversity of plant life: we are told that there are some half a million different types of plants. God did not want to make a boring and monotonous creation by any means indeed! He instead lavishly provided for not only the aesthetic appeal of his creation but also for the needs of all his creatures. With almost seven billion persons needing food on this planet today, the land has produced so bountifully that there is no reason why any should suffer hunger for lack of food.

Note, at this point, there is no mention of eating meat. The plants of the field were able to supply enough food so it was possible to survive without eating meat. Likewise, the fruit trees produced not only their fruit to eat but also seed for their own continuance and preservation in the created order established by God.

III.   Our Lord Created the Sun, Moon, and Stars (Gen. 1:14–19)

In God's fourth workday, he created the heavenly bodies, as verse 16 tells us: "God made two great lights—the greater light to govern the day and the lesser light to govern the night." To avoid any possible notions of worshiping these astral bodies, notice the writer deliberately holds back from referring to them as the "sun" and the "moon" by their Hebrew names; instead, he uses this circumlocution of the "greater and lesser lights."

But what a wonder these two bodies are. The sun is the center of our solar system, yet located some 93 million miles from us it serves as the gravitational center of our whole solar system. It is just far enough away from us to send us the heat we need, but not indeed any closer, for in that case it would imperil life. And the moon, some 232,000 miles away from us, yet it, too, serves us well, waxing and waning in its lesser reflected light from the sun. Thus the earth revolves around the sun every 365 1/4 days, tilted on its own axis of 23 1/3 degrees, as the moon revolves around the earth. What magnificent bodies God has put into orbit through the work of his fingers, functioning so flawlessly without any "recalls" on the performance of either body or the need for any replacement parts.

God also "made the stars" (v. 16), a comment almost made as an aside. But what a work beyond description or our comprehension, for in our own Milky Way Galaxy alone, there are some two hundred billion stars! In addition, God made two hundred billion other galaxies! How vast and how staggering is the immensity of these galaxies, for even though the stars number perhaps even more than in the billions of trillions, the prophet Isaiah taught that God called each star out each night by its own name (Isa. 40:26). If God knows some trillions of stars by name, it is no huge task for him to know each of the small number approaching a mere seven billion persons on earth by name!

IV.   Our Lord Created All Animal Life (Gen. 1:20–25)

In verse 21 we come to the creation of animal life: "So God created the great creatures of the sea and every living and moving thing with which the waters teem." With God's great fifth act of creation, there are several steps, or stages, to the divine work. First, God made the birds of the air (v. 20); then, he made the fish of the sea (v. 21); followed by his creation of the animals on land (v. 25).

A most important clause now appears, for the creatures of the sea, every winged bird, and every wild animal or livestock was made "according to its kind" (vv. 24a, 24c, 25a, 25b, 25c). The word "kind" is not defined scientifically, so as to make it equal to species, genus, family, or order, but the term does refer to the genetic stability of all that God made. Despite the extreme complexity of the DNA molecule, this double helix has a blueprint for life that is structured so that like begets like. While the classification systems for plants and animals used by C. Lynnaeus (1707–1776) and G. L. Buffon (1707–1788) are meant to describe, they are not in themselves predictive and therefore definitive systems. But if someone is thinking "according to its kind" can be stretched to indicate what the evolutionary theory of "natural selection" argued for—namely, that this system can yield changes and mutations across kingdom, phyla, or class—neither the biblical nor scientific data offer sufficient evidence that can complete the case for such major jumps that support evolutionary theory.

If we are amazed at the variety in plant and tree life with its half a million varieties, what shall we say about some seven million kinds of specimens from the animal world? God must have enjoyed himself as he gave us plenty of diversity and variety in forms.

V.   OUR LORD CREATED ALL HUMAN LIFE (GEN. 1:26–31)

Not only are humans the final work of God, but they represent the highest mark reached for all six of the creative actions. Verse 26 reads: "Then God said, 'Let us make mankind in our image, in our likeness, and let them rule over the fish of the sea and the birds in the sky, over the livestock and all the wild animals, and over all the creatures that move along the ground.'"

The phrase that emphasizes the fact that we have now reached the zenith of all creation appears in the description that the man and the woman are made in God's "own image." Verse 27 repeats this teaching: "So God created man in his own image, in the image of God he created him; male and female he created them." Sea life, birds, wild animals and livestock had all been created "according to its kind" (vv. 21, 24, 25), but humanity is now made in "the image of God."

What is this "image of God"? It surely does not refer to the physical shape of mortals, for God is spirit and therefore does not possess physicality (John 4:24; Isa. 31:3). However, the mortals who have been given the task of subduing the created order have had trouble subduing themselves ever since sin entered the world. This is why the "image of God" includes our ability to speak, our ability to love, our ability to "have dominion" over the created order (but with accountability to our Creator), and the gift of knowledge.

In retrospect, one cannot help noticing the restraint and careful reserve with which this narrative of creation is given to us here. How graciously God has provided for men and women, and yet the amazing variety and diversity is passed over as if it were not all that big of a deal to the Creator himself. But we who now enjoy all of this extravagance can only thank our heavenly Father for all his blessings.

The emphasis falls on the action of God. The whole narrative is told in high-style prose, with emphasis on refrains such as, "And evening came to pass, and morning came to pass" (literal translation mine, vv. 5b, 8b, 13b,

19, 23, 31), or "God saw that it was good" (vv. 4, 10b, 18, 25b, 31), with clear definitions of "day," "night," and the like.

What about the time it took to create the world? Actually, the text does not focus on the time element. To be sure, it is not beyond divine ability to create the whole universe in a matter of milliseconds. But if that is so, what do we make of Exodus 20:8–11, which could be accurately rendered: "Remember the day of the Sabbath, by keeping it holy. In the space of six days you are to cultivate and work all your labor . . . for in the space of six days the Lord worked on the sky and the land, the sea and all that is in them."[2] The point is that the traditional "in six days" translation is better rendered as an adverbial accusative of extent of time signifying "over the course of six days."

God does not create "days" until the fourth "day," thus the first three "days" are not measured by our sun and moon. Moreover, the seventh "day" does not have the standard refrain, "evening and morning," so it continues to the present day as God has "rested" from all his creative labors (Heb. 4:1–3).

Conclusions

1. God made the world out of nothing (*creatio ex nihilo*) according to John 1:1–3; Genesis 1:1, and Hebrews 11:3, which states: "By faith we understand that the universe was formed at God's command, so that what is seen was not made of what was visible."
2. There was an absolute beginning to the world prior to which only God existed.
3. God created by the spoken word of his power (Gen. 1:3, 6, 9, 11, 14, 20, 24, 26). The psalmist agreed: "By the word of the Lord the heavens were made, their starry hosts by the breath of his mouth. . . . For he spoke, and it came to be; he commanded, and it stood firm" (Ps. 33:6, 9).
4. Everything that came from the hand of God was "very good."

---

² C. John Collins, "Reading Genesis 1:1–2:3 as an Act of Communication: Discourse Analysis and Literal Interpretation," in *Did God Create in 6 Days?* eds. Joseph A. Pipa Jr., and David W. Hall (Powder Springs, GA: Tolle Lege Press, 1995), 141.

5. At the pinnacle of God's creative work is the fact that men and women are made in the image of God.

STUDY QUESTIONS AND DISCUSSION STARTERS

1. What clues are given in Genesis 1:1 that the first phrase ("in the beginning") should be interpreted as an absolute beginning for the universe? Of what importance is this fact for the doctrine of creation?
2. While the verb "to create" (Hebrew *bara*) does not mean "to create out of nothing," this concept can be found in other passages in the New Testament and elsewhere. Can you name where those passages might be, and what they say?
3. How do you explain verse 2 of Genesis 1? Did God originally make the world dark, formless, and empty? How do these fit into the story of creation then?
4. What method did God use in creating the world, despite the fact that all too many say that Genesis and the Bible do not teach us anything about "how" God created the world? What problem does God creating "light" first in verse 3 raise with what we are told on day 4, and what is the best resolution to this problem?

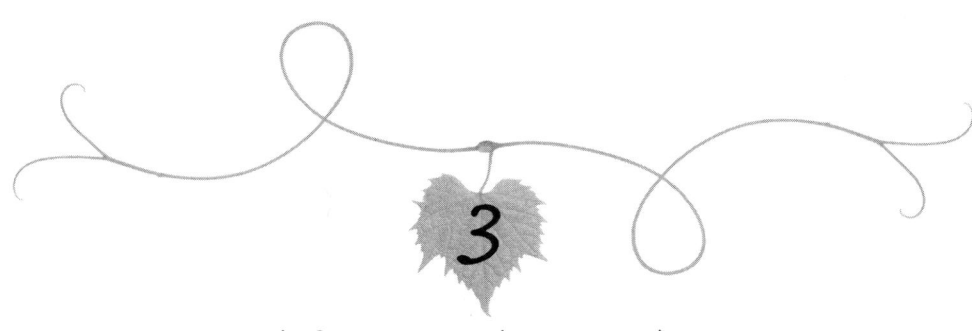

A Garden for Adam and Eve

Genesis 2:4–25

Walter C. Kaiser Jr.

G enesis 2:4–25 appear as if a new or second account of the creation narrative is about to begin. For having just completed the creation narrative in chapter 1 of Genesis, the impression is that all of a sudden we are in a time when plants, animals, and people had not yet been created as had been claimed to have happened on the third day in the narrative as Genesis 1:11–12. Is this an alternate creation account? Or is this a contradiction between two accounts? What is the solution to this apparent or real problem?

It is true that the two narratives use two different names for God. Genesis 1 uses Elohim some thirty-five times and Genesis 2–3 uses Yahweh Elohim as a compound name some nineteen times instead. There are other differences as well, but this is enough to get us started.

But this suggestion that there are two accounts of creation here fails to note that the account in Genesis 1 gives us the overall picture of creation in its totality, while the second narrative gives to us a more graphic set of details from the same creation account. However, these details are specifically limited to the setting of the garden of Eden. Therefore, instead of concluding that there are two accounts of creation in these chapters, the first one more sober and simple in its structure and details (Gen. 1) with the other being more colorful and filled with literary imagination (Gen. 2), a good case can be made instead for giving the first account as the story of the whole universe, with a progress report of the special preparations God made for the first human couple in the garden of Eden in chapter 2.

Concerning the alleged divergence between Genesis 1:11–12 and the account in Genesis 2:5–9 and 19, the reference in Genesis 2 is not to the first creation of plants and animals but to the order of events in the preparation of what was to appear in the garden of Eden. Moreover, the plants that Genesis 2 refers to were distinctly named as the "thorns (or shrubs) of the field" and the "grain of the field" (2:5 NASB). Neither of these two expressions denote the vegetable kingdom in general, which is what Genesis 1 talks about. Rather, here the Hebrew word *siah* refers to the thorns or thistles or shrubs of the field, and the Hebrew word *'eseb* points to the grain, wheat, or barley of the field, all of which are in a separate category not mentioned in Genesis 1.

Two reasons are given for the absence of thorns and grain in the garden of Eden: "[because] the Lord God had not sent rain on the earth" and "[because] there was no one to work the ground" (2:5). This is a distinctive mark from what appears in Genesis 1.

In the first chapter of Genesis, Scripture stresses that plants and trees naturally reproduce themselves by seed placed within each plant or tree, but these plants in the garden of Eden need something else in order to thrive. Thus, all species of grain, while isolated specimens might exist here and there in the wild by themselves, would not be nurtured or cultivated until there was a man who would care for the soil. Conversely, thorns and thistles of the field would not propagate their own seeds, or grow fresh plants, until it rained.

Accordingly, after man's fall in the garden, Adam was compelled to till the ground, and as the rains came down, thorns and thistles spread out across the fields along with cultivated fields of wheat, oats, and barley.

Focal Point:	v. 8 "Now the Lord God had planted a garden in the east, in Eden; and there he put the man he had formed."
Homiletical Keyword:	Works

Interrogative: What?
                              (What are the works of God
                              as he prepared a garden for
                              the first couple?)

I.   GOD CREATES A MAN AND A GARDEN (GEN. 2:4B–9)
  A.   NO SHRUB OF THE FIELD OR PLANT OF THE FIELD (2:4–6)
  B.   MAN IS FORMED FROM THE DUST OF THE GROUND (2:7)
  C.   ONE GARDEN WITH TWO TREES (2:8–9)

II.   GOD PROVIDES IRRIGATION FOR THE GARDEN (GEN. 2:10–14)

III. GOD CREATES AN EQUAL BEING SUITED TO MAN (GEN. 2:15–25)
  A.   WORKING AND CARING FOR THE GARDEN (2:15–17)
  B.   THE GIFT OF A BRIDE (2:18–25)
  C.   COMMENTATOR'S ESTIMATE (2:24–25)

I.   GOD CREATES A MAN AND A GARDEN (GEN. 2:4B–9)

The narrative in Genesis 2 is neither a flashback, that is, a retelling
of the story of Genesis 1, nor is it a completely different version of the
original creation episode. Instead, it is a parallel description of God's most
distinctive special preparation of a garden called Eden and an introduction of its first occupants.

Verse 4 has the first of ten appearances in the book of Genesis of the
rubric: "This is the account of," which in this case it goes on to add: "the
heavens and the earth when they were created" (5:1 [for a variant of the for-
mula]; 6:9; 10:1; 11:10, 27; 25:12, 19; 36:1, 9; 37:2). Many translations and
commentators divide 2:4 into two parts, making 2:4a go with chapter 1
and 2:4b go with the garden of Eden account. But that division seems to be
unnecessary, for each account forms a unique part of the continuing story
of how God went about creating not only the universe but also the first
residence for the first couple in Eden; both were essential parts of the story.

We are also aware of the fact that we suddenly shift from the name
Elohim, "God," in Genesis 1 to "Lord God" (Hebrew *Yahweh 'lohim*) in
chapters 2–3, which appears some nineteen times; it is a combination that

appears only once more in the rest of the whole Pentateuch (Exod. 9:30), and about twenty more times in the rest of the Bible. This double name, however, is to be distinguished from another double name in the Hebrew: *'adonay Yahweh*, which is used almost exclusively in the Abrahamic covenant (Gen. 15:2, 8) and in the Davidic covenant (2 Sam. 7:18, 19, 20, 22, 28, 29). However, those scholars who have put forth the theory that the compound name "Lord God" is the result of an amalgamation of sources (such as is used in literary-critical source theory of E, J, or P documents—a favorite scholarly theory that devised a number of imaginary documents to be the sources that lay behind our present biblical text) is a theory that often exhibits the fact that it lacks wide reading experience in ancient Near Eastern materials, for in the Near Eastern documents the alternative names for God are routinely used in order to gain parallelism of terms in the Semitic poetic or prose lines. Therefore, the multiple names for a deity should not be read as a betrayal of the fact that the source or document from which that portion of the material came used only one of those divine names. Based on the Near Eastern materials, that hypothesis has now been shown to be faulty.

A.   NO SHRUB OF THE FIELD OR PLANT OF THE FIELD (2:4–6)

The Hebrew text begins in 2:4b with "in the day (*beyom*) when the Lord God made the heavens and the earth." This "day" did not specify a period of twelve hours, or twenty-four hours, but it is an idiom much like our expression "in the hour that" or the "day (or time) of the horse and buggy." This does not mean an hour of sixty minutes or even a day of twenty-four hours in length. Rather, it too is much like Numbers 3:1, which mentions "in the day" (Hebrew *beyom*) that "the Lord spoke to Moses on Mount Sinai." Recall that Moses was on the Mount for forty days and forty nights, so that "day" in this instance encompassed at least forty days and nights! (cf. Num. 7:84; 2 Sam 22:1, also in Ps. 18:1, where *yom* is used in the Hebrew text).

The scene traced in 2:5–7, however, is often prematurely declared to be a flat contradiction to 1:11–12, which describes vegetation as being created on the third workday of creation, three days before the creation of man. But in 2:5–7, the creation of plants and the humans are closely linked in the timing of their appearance! However, this judgment is premature because 2:5–7 does not say just when it was that God created man in the Eden narrative. Moreover, if it is such a straightforward inconsistency, why did the writer (or redactor) do nothing to smooth it out, but instead left what is assumed in modern times to be a blatant contradiction standing almost side by side in the two chapters? This objection, it must be said, also fails to notice that the shrubs (thorns and thistles) and grains mentioned here are separate and different from other seed-bearing forms of plants that do not necessarily need human cultivation or the presence of rain to encourage their growth. Moreover, 2:5 anticipates 3:18, where thorns and thistles were a result of the fall, and human cultivation was necessary for engaging in grain farming.

But the scene has not been painted for us as one that features arid or desert conditions. Even though rain has not yet come on the earth, the Hebrew text says that an *'ed* rises from the ground (v. 6) to water the earth's surface in the garden. This Hebrew word appears only one other time (Job 36:27), but it is unusual in that in Genesis 2 it goes *up* from the earth, whereas rivers generally go down. Therefore, this may be something like a mist or dew that rose from the ground, or a foggy dew that settled over the land, which is a suggestion that finds some support from a possible Sumerian cognate for "dew."

The long sentence of 4b–7 in Hebrew (containing a protasis in 4b, then a series of circumstantial clauses in 5–6, and finally an apodosis in verse 7) climaxes with the Lord God "forming" (Hebrew *yatsar*) man from the dust of the ground. This man will be the focus of the text's attention.

B.   MAN IS FORMED FROM THE DUST OF THE GROUND (2:7)

Genesis 1:27 simply asserted that "God created mankind in his own image," but no further details were given. Genesis 2:7 will now supply those further details: "The Lord God formed man from the dust of the ground." The Hebrew uses the literary device of assonance, saying something like "God formed an *earthling* from the *earth,*" for the word for "man" in Hebrew is *'adam* and the word for "ground" is *'adamah*. The action of God is likened to that of a potter, for the passage uses the same Hebrew verb *yotser,* meaning "to form, to shape," which is used elsewhere for the work of a potter (2 Sam. 17:28; Isa. 29:16; Jer. 18:2, 3, 4). Of course, a potter works with mud or clay, not dust, therefore the emphasis may not be an exact parallel of the work a potter engages in, but instead from the dust of the ground, God is able to bring the dust to life as he adds vitality and life to his work. The language is indeed figurative, for God is spirit and is not corporeal, thus his work of formation must come instead from his verbal orders as Genesis 1 stressed. Nevertheless, the use of the word "dust" only enhances the work of God all the more, for man is raised from the lowliness (as well as the dryness) of the dust to be a creature made in God's image. That is more than our rags-to-riches stories; it is a narrative of being raised from nonexistence to potentially becoming one of the sons (and later in Eve's case one of the daughters) of the living God.

The remainder of verse 7 shows that this human is without life until the breath of God is breathed into his nostrils; at that point he can become "alive," which is the best way to translate the Hebrew *nefesh hayyah*. At this point the expression does not speak of Adam as having a "soul" (some rendered this expression as "living soul," as if to speak about Adam's possessing a spiritual portion to his person). Instead, it simply signified that whereas he previously had been inert and dead as the dust on the ground, he now, with the infusion of the breath of God, was "alive!" This would seem to rule out God's using any previously existing animate forms of life to form or shape Adam's body, or that dust was perhaps a figure of speech for some previously existing animal form, for he never was alive until God breathed the breath of life into him! That is when Adam became animate and living!

C.   ONE GARDEN WITH TWO TREES (2:8–9)

The figurative depiction of God changes at this point, from his work being similar to that of a potter to his now taking on the figure of a gardener as he plants a garden in Eden (v. 8). The meaning of the term *Eden* is often connected to the Sumerian-Akkadian *edinu*, meaning a "plain, prairie, or flatland." In Hebrew the word related to Eden occurs only one other time, in Nehemiah 9:25, where it is used to mean "to delight oneself." The word may also be related to the term for "pleasure" in Genesis 18:12. The word "Eden" in its singular or plural form occurs some fifteen times in the Old Testament as a designation for a place. Other parallel expressions for Eden are the "garden of Yahweh" (Gen. 13:10; Isa. 51:3) or "the garden of God" (Ezek. 28:13; 31:9). This is not to imply that this is the place where Yahweh lives, but that he was the garden's planter and preparer, not necessarily its occupant.

Note that the emphasis is not on the fact that the garden was only a paradise, or a place of blissful enjoyment; instead, man is placed in the garden "to work it and take care of it" (2:15). Moreover, the text focuses on the trees of the garden more than anything else.

There were especially two trees of note in this garden: "the tree of life" and "the tree of the knowledge of good and evil" (v. 9), both of which were placed in the midst of the garden, meaning among the other trees of the garden, rather than necessarily projecting a spot in the dead center of that space. This second tree of the knowledge of good and evil appears only here in the whole Bible, that is, Genesis 2:9, 17. But the other tree, the tree of life, can be found in Genesis 3:22, 24 and Proverbs 3:18; 11:30; 13:12; 15:4, as well as in the New Testament in Revelation 2:7 and 22:2, 14, 19. Apparently, God will re-create this tree of life in an existence similar to the garden of Eden later on in the eschaton of those last days in the new heavens and new earth.

The tree of the knowledge of good and evil, however, becomes the focal point of our narrative. The explanation for good and evil has a moral sense that tends to bracket all human experience, but this is not to conclude, as some Roman Catholic interpreters do, that the morality talked about here has a bearing specifically on one's sexual life, for that interpretation misses the obvious point that the woman has not yet been created. Furthermore, in 3:22, it would need to apply sexuality to God, for when the man and the woman ate of the tree, it said, "the man has now become like one of us."

In fact, the author does not pause to explain the meaning of this tree, for he assumes the man will know exactly what is intended. Moreover, one does not need to experience all good and all evil in order to know what it is. What God wanted to prevent, by refusing the fruit of this tree to his humans, was moral autonomy and a freedom that was more like anarchy. It was not that there were certain enzymes in the fruit of this tree any more than there are similar dangerous contents in the Eucharist celebrated by the church. Nevertheless, there are warnings about eating and drinking the body and blood of the Lord in an unworthy manner, for if one is not careful, it will make one sick, and some have even died as a result of disregarding this warning (1 Cor. 11:27–29). God did not want mortals deciding for themselves what was good and what was bad. Humans become their own gods when they make the rules for their morality; we think we have become sovereign gods to ourselves when we initiate our own rules!

II.   GOD PROVIDES IRRIGATION FOR THE GARDEN (GEN. 2:10–14)

Some think that on the basis of this section, it is possible to locate the garden of Eden in the ancient Near East. Alas, such a state of affairs is not at all possible. To be sure, the names of the third river, the Hiddekel (or Tigris) River, as well as the name of the fourth river, the Euphrates River, are well known to us today, as they were then in Mesopotamia. But we are at an absolute loss to define the Pishon and the Gihon Rivers despite many interesting suggestions.

The Gihon River (v. 13) reminds us of the Gihon Spring that supplies water to Jerusalem at the base of the city of Jerusalem (1 Kings 1:33, 38, 45; 2 Chron. 32:30; 33:14), yet according to Genesis 2:13 this river "winds through the entire land of Cush." Normally, the Old Testament uses the word "Cush" to refer to Nubia and Ethiopia, a region of the Upper (i.e., southern) Nile River. There is another reference to Cush, meaning the land of the Kassites, located east of the Tigris River, but that too is far from Jerusalem.

The situation with regard to the Pishon River (vv. 11–12) is even more difficult. It encompasses the entire land of Havilah, where there is gold. Havilah is both a designation for a location and a people (Gen. 10:29; 1 Chron. 1:23), thus it reflects an ethnic tradition of peoples living on both sides of the Red Sea. We are told of gold coming from countries to the south and brought to both Egypt and Israel from Put, or Ophir. But neither of these two locations has absolutely been identified either. The only thing we know for sure is that "the gold of that land is good" (v. 12), and that aromatic resin and onyx are also found there. We have also found a shipping receipt near Tel-Aviv on an ostracon saying "gold from Ophir."

III.   GOD CREATES AN EQUAL BEING SUITED TO MAN (GEN. 2:15–25)

A.   *WORKING AND CARING FOR THE GARDEN (2:15–17)*

God placed Adam in the garden of Eden "to work it and take care of it" (v. 15). Involved in his tending was the idea of protecting (Hebrew *shamar*) it, for that was the basic idea of the Hebrew root. It is the same verb used in 3:24, where the cherubs were on guard to protect access to the tree of life in the garden, after the human couple was expelled. Notice that human toil and work was not the consequence of sin, for this injunction to work preceded the fall into sin.

There was just one simple prohibition: "you must not eat from the tree of the knowledge of good and evil, for when you do eat of it you will surely die" (v. 17). The death they would suffer was immediate spiritual death followed (apparently later on) by physical death. True, Adam lived to be 930 years old (Gen. 5:5), yet he, who was built to be immortal, became mortal along with all of his descendants. So physical death followed spiritual death!

B.   THE GIFT OF A BRIDE (2:18–25)

So far, everything that has been scrutinized by God he had judged to be "good," or "very good"; but now, for the first time, we are told that something "is not good" (v. 18a). Man was not meant to be alone, and, in 1:31, it was only after woman has been formed that God pronounces everything "very good." This is not a human judgment, but a divine estimate of the situation.

But God not only evaluates the situation; he decides to rectify it by making a "helper suitable for him" (v. 18b). The Hebrew word for "helper" is *'ezer,* which is a strong word, since it frequently appears as a title for God (Exod. 18:4; Deut. 33:7, 26, 29; Ps. 33:20; 115:9–11; 124:8; 146:5, etc.), who is called our "Helper." However, there is a related term in Ugaritic, the early Canaanite language that shares about 60 percent of its vocabulary with Hebrew. It is the word *'gezer,* meaning "power" or "authority," which we can now add to the expression that follows it in Hebrew: "corresponding to" or "equal to" the man.[1] Originally, Hebrew had at this place in its thirty-letter alphabet two laryngeals, an *'ayin* and a *'gayin.* The two letters fell together morphologically over time, but we know from older proper names that one of them had at one time a "*g*" sound as is preserved in the names of "Gaza" or "Gomorrah," both presently spelled in Hebrew today merely with the *'ayin,* but which at one time must have begun with a *'gayin.* Therefore, the term meant that God

---

[1] Walter C. Kaiser Jr., "Correcting Caricatures: The Biblical Teaching on Women," *Priscilla Papers* 19, no. 2 (2005): 5–11.

created not a "helper" for Adam, but a "power or authority" that would correspond to him!

The way God did this was to cause Adam to fall into a deep sleep (v. 21). While he was sleeping, God took a portion from the man's side and built a woman from this original piece. After he finished "building" the woman, he brought her to Adam (v. 22). Previous to this, Adam had been given the task of naming each living creature in creation (vv. 19–20), but none of them suited his concept of what a companion should be like, for he turned them all down as potential partners!

However, when God finished building Eve, he brought her to the man and his joy and happiness were ecstatic beyond measure. He cried out, "Now, at last [Hebrew *happa`am*], this is bone of my bone and flesh of my flesh; she shall be called woman, for she was taken out of man" (v. 23, my translation). The expression "bone of my bone and flesh of my flesh" indicates family propinquity, that is, an expression that generally means that she was formed from the same roots or the same family.

C.   COMMENTATOR'S ESTIMATE *(2:24–25)*

The man was to sever one relationship, that is, the one he had with his family, and a new one he must now commence. The most crucial element in this marriage is to be found in the verbs, where one former relationship was to be forsaken and the new one in marriage was to be clung to. Now the man and the woman were to become one flesh (v. 24b), which spoke most clearly about their solidarity. Adam by himself was not one flesh, neither was Eve by herself one flesh; but together they were one flesh.

Finally, there was an absence of shame, for both of them were naked, yet they felt no shame (v. 25). Later in the Old Testament, nakedness will everywhere else be a form of defenselessness and shame, yet at this stage in the relationship of Adam and Eve there were no barriers of any kind, including any sort of self-consciousness, but a complete and unhindered giving and enjoying of one another. However, as soon as sin enters their lives, that open, unbashful, and un-self-conscious state disappears. The issue of nakedness will arise again, however, after the self-assertion of the woman and the man against God (3:10).

Conclusions

1. Human beings enjoy vitality and life because God breathed into the first man the breath of life. Before that they were as inert as the dust of the ground!
2. The woman was made as an authority or power equal to the man in order to be his companion and to ward off loneliness and to form a solidarity of one flesh with him.
3. God gave the garden of Eden to Adam in order that he might tend it and care for it, showing that the doctrine of work precedes the fall and that work was meant to be enjoyed, not countered as a drudgery!
4. The solidarity and unity of the man and woman were intended from the beginning to be a source of unbounded joy for both of them without shame or a sense of self-consciousness.

Study Questions and Discussion Starters

1. What is the alleged divergence between Genesis 1:11–12 and Genesis 2:5–9, 19? What is the best answer to this complaint found in the discussion in this book?
2. What are the two reasons given in Genesis 2:5 for the absence of thorns (or shrubs) of the field and the grain of the field?
3. Discuss the rubric, or the heading, found some ten times in the book of Genesis that began in 2:4. How does that rubric affect our understanding as to how the book of Genesis may have originated or been put together?
4. What is the explanation for the meaning and the switch from the divine name of *Elohim* ("God") used some thirty-five times in Genesis 1 to the use of the divine name of *Yahweh Elohim* ("Lord God") used some nineteen times in Genesis 2–3, when this later name for God appears only one more time in any of the first five books of the Old Testament?
5. Some argue that the use of "dust of the ground" in Genesis 2:7 could be a symbol or an image of the fact that God used preexisting animal forms as the substance from which man emerged by means of natural selection. How could you use the fact that the

Bible teaches that man did not become alive until God breathed into his nostrils the breath of life to refute this argument?

6. The tree of the knowledge of good and evil did not claim to embody certain enzymes in the fruit of this tree, but as explained in these lessons, this tree was used in a similar way to the bread and wine are used in Christian theology. What is that Christian institution, and how are its elements similar to those of this tree?

7. Since God placed Adam in the garden of Eden to work it and take care of it, what does this say about a doctrine of work prior to the fall?

8. What difference does it make if Eve is made to be a helper suitable for Adam or a power equal to him, as described in Genesis 2:18–25?

9. What concept is taught about marriage as Adam and Eve are brought together to be one flesh (2:24b)?

A Divine Ode to Creation

Psalm 104

Walter C. Kaiser Jr.

Strolling along Fifth Avenue in New York City, heading from midtown toward downtown, visitors are astounded at the incredible steel and concrete structure rising up in front of them. They can't help but stop and bend their necks skyward, peering up in awe at a building so massive, so tall, soaring to the very heavens, it appears. It is December 1930 and the finishing touches are being applied to what will soon be the world's tallest building (1,250 feet and 102 floors) when it opens on May 1, 1931. Little wonder that the Empire State Building, constructed in just one year and forty-five days, was later dubbed one of the seven wonders of the modern world. Dwarfing all competitors, the tower held preeminence for four decades until eventually surpassed by other skyscrapers.

In Psalm 104 we encounter the one and only God who does not need to scrape the sky in Babelesque fashion to make a name for himself. Indeed, the Creator Lord made the skies and all the wonders therein and beyond. As such, the psalmist in Psalm 104 paints for us a living image of the order, goodness, and power that God has placed in his creation, where it could be said that he is described as the "Lord of seven wonders!" One creative wonder follows another, much as it did in Genesis 1—the sky (vv. 2–4), the earth (vv. 5–9), the water (vv. 10–13), vegetation (vv. 14–18), the moon and the sun (vv. 19–23), the sea (vv. 24–26), and the gift of life (vv. 27–30), followed by an anthem of praise to the maker of all things (vv. 31–35).

The main outline for this psalm, then, essentially follows the same order of events of the creation narrative found in Genesis 1. As the psalmist meditated on the content of Genesis 1, he found joy and inspiration for composing this psalm. However, that does not mean that this psalm is a mere copy of the original narrative in Genesis, for it has an originality and a force all its own. In some ways, this psalm presents the material of creation in an even more striking form, exhibiting the infinite greatness of the work of the Creator's hands.

Genesis portrays the beginning of the created order, but this psalm goes beyond the account of what took place in the past and depicts what is an ongoing and continued living demonstration found in the created order. Genesis contains the record of creation, but the psalm exhibits the animation of creation. Genesis is a still-life picture, while the psalm is full of movement and graceful beauty.

J. J. Stewart Perowne continued this line of thought in even grander expressions:

> How vivid are the images which it calls up—the wild ass roaming the sands of the wilderness, stooping to slake his thirst at the stream which God has provided; the birds building their nests, and breaking forth into song in the trees which fringe the margin of the torrent-beds; the wild goats bounding from rock to rock, and finding their home in the inaccessible crags; the young lions filling the forest at night with their roar, and "seeking from God their prey"; and the sea with the same plentitude of life, its depths peopled with huge monsters and swarming myriads of lesser fish, and its surface studded with sails, the image of the enterprise, the traffic, the commerce of the world; and lastly, in fine contrast with this merely animal activity of creatures led by their appetites, the even tenor, the calm unobtrusiveness of man's daily life of labour: take all these together, and we have a picture which for truth and depth of colouring, for animation, tenderness, beauty, has never been surpassed.[1]

While the psalm is without indisputable strophe divisions, its main outline follows the first chapter of Genesis. Therefore, its divisions look something like this:

---

[1] J. J. Stewart Perowne, *The Book of Psalms*, vol. 2 (1878 reprint; Grand Rapids: Zondervan, 1966), 233.

Day 1, Genesis 1:3–5: the sky with its light (Ps. 104:2–4)

Day 2, Genesis 1:6–8: the "firmament" divides the waters (Ps. 104:5–9)

Day 3a, Genesis 1:9–10: the gift of water (Ps. 104:10–13)

Day 3b, Genesis 1:11–13: vegetation and trees (Ps. 104:14–18)

Day 4, Genesis 1:14–19: luminaries as timekeepers (Ps. 104:19–23)

Day 5, Genesis 1:20–23: creatures of the sea and air (Ps. 104:25–26)

Day 6a, Genesis 1:24–28: animals and man (Ps. 104:27)

Day 6b, Genesis 1:29–31: food appointed for all (Ps. 104:27–30)[2]

Let us, then, use the same structure as an outline for our teaching, preaching, or personal study of this text. In fact, the great hymn of Sir Robert Grant, entitled "O Worship the King," derived its origin from this psalm, but its meter came from William Kethe's sixteenth-century paraphrase, "My soul, praise the Lord" ("the Old 104th").[3]

Focal Point:	v. 24
	"How many are your works, Lord! In wisdom you made them all; the earth is full of your creatures."
Homiletical Keyword:	Evidence
Interrogative:	What? (What is the evidence of the works of God in all the world?)

INTRODUCTION (Ps. 104:1)

I.   "LET THERE BE LIGHT" (Ps. 104:2A)

II. "LET THERE BE AN EXPANSE . . . TO SEPARATE THE WATER" (Ps. 104:2B–9)

III. "LET THE WATER BE GATHERED TOGETHER . . . AND THE DRY LAND APPEAR" (Ps. 104:10–13)

---

[2] Derek Kidner, *Psalms 73–150*, Tyndale Commentary (London: Inter-Varsity, 1975), 368. This outline is similar to Perowne, 234.

[3] Kidner, Psalms 73–150, 368.

IV.   "Let the Land Produce Vegetation" (Ps. 104:14–18)

V.   "Let There Be Lights in the Expanse . . . to Separate Day and Night" (Ps. 104:19–23)

VI.   "Let the Waters Teem . . . and Let the Birds Fly" (Ps. 104:24–26)

VII.   "Let the Land Produce Living Creatures. . . . Let Us Make Man" (Ps. 104:27–30)

VIII.   A Prayer for the Glory of God Enduring Forever (Ps. 104:31–35)

Introduction (Ps. 104:1)

Though the Septuagint (LXX) had a headline that claimed it for David, this untitled psalm calls for a praise coming forth from the psalmist's soul, both in its exordium and conclusion. So great are the works of God that they called forth a response from the psalmist's whole being.

To be sure, there are striking resemblances at several points to the Egyptian Pharaoh Akhenaton's "Hymn to Aton" (Egyptian sun god, circa 14th century BC), particularly in its description of the provisions for the beasts and the birds (vv. 11–14), provisions for the creatures of the day and the night (vv. 19–23), and the sea with its ships (vv. 25–26). Except for these somewhat trivial points of contact, the two poems go off to develop their own distinctive thoughts. The "Hymn to Aton" focuses on the mystery of birth, the plurality of races, and the distant lands, while the biblical psalm takes its structure and general outline from Genesis 1. The Egyptian text worships the sun, but Genesis worships Yahweh, the maker and Creator of all that exists.

I.   "Let There Be Light" (Ps. 104:2a)

At the beginning of creation, the voice of God initiated it all by saying, "Let there be light" (Gen. 1:3–5). But for the psalmist, who connects a series of participial clauses with what precedes, regards this creation as a continual work of God in creation. God "clothes himself," or "apparels himself," with light. That in itself is not as surprising as it might seem, for in the revelation that comes later on in the New Testament, we are told that "God is light" (1 John 1:5; also John 1:4–9). In making light as if it were his robe, even though God is invisible, nevertheless his glory is readily evident. Our Lord is said to dwell in light inaccessible, yet his glory is still radiated throughout the whole world.

How foolish it would be to seek God in his physical person, for God is spirit and not flesh. Yet he has mercifully allowed us to see his majesty and magnificence in the evidence of his presence manifested in his creative glory. How awesome and altogether worthy is the Lord of glory to be clothed with light as his robe!

II. "Let There Be An Expanse . . . to Separate The Water" (Ps. 104:2b–9)

The work of the second day is now celebrated in verses 2b–9. First, God "spread out the heavens like a curtain" (my translation), a figure that also appears in Isaiah 40:22 (cf. Isa. 42:5; 44:24). The heavens are called an expanse, or in the Latin Vulgate and Septuagint, a "firmament." However, the Hebrew *raqia`* does not carry the connotation of a solid dome or a hardened canopy over the earth, as if it were one of our modern domed football stadiums, as some contemporary commentators like to describe it. On the contrary, it means it was simply an expanse or a platform.

This expanse was spread out so as to separate the waters that were in the skies from the waters that were below these heavens. In this sense, the heavens acted as a separating curtain, which was likened to a tent. God is represented as daily spreading out this tent of his, which functioned as a place of safety and repose. Some of the church fathers observed that the tent was used, not to show us the form that the heavens took, but to show with what ease God works, for it is as easy for God to stretch out the heavenly tent as it is for a Bedouin in the Near East to stretch out the animal skins that form the place of his abode.

In verse 3 the figure of a beam is used to describe the shaping of the rooms in God's abode in heaven. But again, it is not the material of God's abode that is offered here, but rather an attempt to meet us in our world, for he gives us pictures suitable for our eyes, just as for our sakes, he put on a robe of light. His chamber was literally the word used for an "upper chamber," built in the Near Eastern culture on the flat roofs of their homes (2 Kings 4:10; Jer. 22:13–14), but built in this case "in the waters" that were above the firmament (Gen. 1:7). What a bold figure of speech! What a magnificent Lord!

Thus, the dizzy heights of the clouds are depicted as the base of God's abode. While this may seem to be insubstantial to us, it is more than adequate for the ethereal lightness of his palace in the heavens.[4] With the "clouds [as] his chariot" and the "beams of his upper chamber" being figurative, it is clear that language has been well nigh exhausted in order to express the relationship of God to our world. But the certain fact is that God dwells in all of his magnificence as the light of the world.

The rendering of the Septuagint better captures verse 4 by taking the original word order of the Hebrew, as did Hebrews 1:7, when it declared "who makes his messengers (or angels) as winds, and his ministers a flaming fire" (my translation). To complete the picture, then, God wraps himself in light, setting up the abode of his tent in heaven, as his angels occasionally take on the form of the wind, lightning, and flashing fire (cf. Ezek. 1:4–7; 10:15). The book of Hebrews argued that angels can be described in these more mundane ways, but the Son himself is addressed as God.

III. "LET THE WATER BE GATHERED TOGETHER . . . AND THE DRY LAND APPEAR" (PS. 104:10–13)

In the third work of creation, there were two great divisions. First, the land and the water were separated (vv. 5–9). Then the earth was clothed with grass, herbs, and trees (vv. 10–18). There is more here than the straightforward statement about the dry land appearing. Instead, we are given a strong emphasis on the Creator's control and a decree that cannot "be moved for ever and ever" (v. 5, my translation). Another metaphor of foundations is used in verse 5, but as Job 26:7 says, God "hung the earth on nothing" (my translation). To insist on a hard, prosaic literalism here is to strain the poetry beyond its intentions, as witnessed by Father Sanchez, who incorrectly relied on such a strong literality in his controversy with Galileo on whether the earth went around the sun or the earth remained firmly planted as the center of our universe. Surely the figures

---

[4] "Ethereal lightness" is a phrase used by Derek Kidner, 369.

of speech in Scripture are to be watched as closely as its literal statements for correct interpretation.

Pagan cosmologies depicted the "deep" (Hebrew *tehom*) as a threat, or as a goddess named Tiamat. However, the alleged derivation of the Hebrew word for "deep" from the Babylonian goddess Tiamat is altogether impossible philologically. Verse 6 describes the deep as the sea that covered or surrounded the earth much as a garment would in a mantle-like fashion. In verses 7–9, the psalmist describes vividly the rise of the continents at the command of God with appropriate boundaries set as God ordained them. Accordingly, the vast, undulating, and tumultuous sea rose and sank with its waves at the rebuke of God, for he confined it to its appointed place.

The boundary (v. 9) separating the sea from the land also appears in Job 38:8–10: "[I] shut up the sea behind doors . . . when I fixed the limits for it." Though verse 9b may seem as if it pertains to Noah's flood, here instead it refers to God's everlasting order that was fixed at creation. God would fix the shoreline and protect the land.

For a moment, the psalmist runs ahead of the Genesis order of creation to excitedly tell us about the hospitable earth that has emerged from the separation of the dry land from the sea. Now that it has dried out, the land itself has under the direction of its Creator become the source of springs and streams of freshwater to supply drink for the beasts of the field (the non-domesticated types, v. 11) and cattle (the domesticated types, v. 14). Meanwhile, the wild donkeys (v. 11b), which are by nature totally independent creatures, who feed themselves, are just like the birds who take care of themselves as well (v. 12). Jesus used the birds as an illustration of his bountiful care in Matthew 6:26; the figure may well have begun here.

God is the one who waters the mountains from the skies above (v. 13a) and he is the one who satisfies the earth "with the fruit of his work," apparently, based on the parallelism, a reference to the rain he sends upon the earth.

IV. "LET THE LAND PRODUCE VEGETATION" (Ps. 104:14–18)

The third workday of creation went on to speak of earth's vegetation and God's making of the trees. With this theme in mind, the psalmist enlarged on this part of the third workday, moving from the wildlife of the last stanza to the domesticated farm animals (v. 14a), and the bread that came from the earth for all to live on (v. 15b).

In addition to the grass that Yahweh grows for the cattle, he also makes the green herbs, which include corn and the grains, to grow for the service of man (v. 14b). The emphasis is on the works of God, for there is nothing to suggest at this point man's cooperation. More than that, God provided wine to make glad the heart of men and oil to make the face of men shine (v. 15a).

The trees of Yahweh (v. 16a) and the cedars of Lebanon (v. 16b) are planted not by mortals but by Yahweh himself. The vine and the olive may require human cultivation, but these trees are different. They are where the large birds, like the stork, built their massive nests, and where the song birds, which are smaller, make their abode (v. 17).

Over against these forests of trees are the high mountains on which the wild goats climb on their crags, and the hyrax (a small, shy rock dweller) lives as well in its steep precipices (v. 18). The environment is suited well for each as planned by God.

V.   "LET THERE BE LIGHTS IN THE EXPANSE . . . TO SEPARATE DAY AND NIGHT" (Ps. 104:19–23)

On the fourth episode of creation, Yahweh set up the rhythm of the greater and lesser lights to illuminate the earth. The moon is mentioned first, for in the Semitic mind, the night preceded the day (v. 19; cf. Gen. 1:14–16).

Night life is depicted as one filled with business and activity as all the beasts of the forest (v. 20b) move out and the young lions roar after their prey (v. 21). The food these animals seek is from God, for he is the source of all that exists. The night is teeming with life and activity. The word "prowl" (or "move") in verse 20 is normally used to describe the movements of reptiles and fish, just as the Hebrew verb appears in Genesis 1:21 and Psalm 69:34 [35] describing the creatures of the sea or the creeping things on the face of the earth, emphasizing their stealthy movements against their prey.

Meanwhile, mortals are resting from their day's labors. However, as the sun rises in the morning, so humans need to ready themselves for their work during the day (v. 23). But the wild animals return to their dens and places of rest awaiting another night of activity (v. 22). In bringing up the topic of man, the psalmist has anticipated the work of the sixth day of creation.

But it was time to pause and take account of all of Yahweh's works. It was time to celebrate the "wisdom" of Yahweh evidenced in all his works, for he had "made them all" (v. 24a), accordingly, "the [whole] earth [was] full of [his] creatures" (v. 24c). The extent of this wealth and riches seen on earth was a barometer of the wealth of the Creator himself. How extensive, how precise, and how unified were all of Yahweh's works shaped and maintained by his wisdom.

VI. "Let the Waters Teem . . . and Let the Birds Fly" (Ps. 104:24–26)

Even though the psalmist had anticipated himself by leaping ahead to describe the birds, beasts, and man himself in the previous section, in these two verses he returns to the fifth day of creation, where God made the "great creatures of the sea and every living and moving thing with which the water teems" (Gen. 1:21).

The sea is one vast ocean of life that ranges from the large forms down to the smallest of life. But in addition to all this sea life, the waters are a virtual highway for the ships of commerce and pleasure to travel (v. 26a).

As for the "leviathan," a name that oftentimes raised a note of alarm among mortals (Ps. 74:13–14), he appears here to portray the large creature as another example of the work of God, all of which glorifies and delights his maker. Some render the thought here as if God made leviathan to play with him, and to have him to sport with, appealing to Job 40:29 [41:5], but while the Jewish tradition supports this rendering, nothing in Scripture supports such a translation.

VII. "Let the Land Produce Living Creatures. . . . Let Us Make Man" (Ps. 104:27–30)

The "spirit" or "breath" of God is essential for the life in all that God has created (v. 30a). This is not a reference to Genesis 2:7, because that inbreathing of the breath of God was confined to the first man alone. Instead, the reference is to Genesis 1:2, where the Holy Spirit is the one who gives life to all. Therefore, in retrospect, God is the source of all life, and he is the one who has maintained life in all its forms on the planet.

Accordingly, all of creation waits on Yahweh to give them their food in its season (v. 27), that is, in the season each needs that particular food in order to be sustained. That is why all the creatures gather as Yahweh opens his hand and satisfies them with good (v. 28). If the Lord should decide to hide his face, the whole creation would be in trouble; the breath of all would be taken away from them and they would die and turn back to dust again (v. 29). The Lord is both the fountain of life and the gracious provider who maintains life itself.

VIII. A Prayer for the Glory of God Enduring Forever (Ps. 104:31–35)

From start to finish, this psalm magnifies the name of the Lord. All of the previous acts of creation exhibit the glory of Yahweh, both now and forever. There are a host of reasons why the Lord ought to rejoice in all his works (v. 31). He is a God awesome in his majesty. One look from him and the earth trembles and shakes in deference to who he is and in respect for what he has made. One touch from him and the mountains are consumed. Moreover, he could, should he have reason to do so, blot out in a moment all the creation he has made (v. 32). Instead, he has decided to maintain all he has created as evidence of his grace and love for all he has made.

Instead of erasing what he has made, here come men and women made in the image of God, who have the gift of singing and recognizing what God has done: "Let us sing to Yahweh as long as [we] live, let us play [our instruments] to our God while we still have our breath and our being" (v. 33, my translation; cf. Ps. 146:2). What is more, let our meditation of our Creator be sweet to him (v. 34), for we who are the climax of his creation, and we who are made in his own image, above all the works of his hand, must use the gifts of speech, song, knowledge, and appreciation to express our unmitigated delight in his person and in everything he has made (v. 34).

The psalm ends with "Hallelujah," that is, "Praise Yah[weh]," for no other word is able to summarize it all. However, one note of sadness must interrupt the proceedings: "let sinners be consumed out of the earth, and let the wicked be no more" (v. 35a–b NASB). Sin had brought discord and introduced disorder into the beautiful order of creation. But the earth can be purified, and harmony can be restored as God can once more pronounce his "very good" on all his creation. It is in this light of the added work of God that the poet blesses and praises Yahweh, as he urges us to do the same, if we have any idea of all that God has done so beautifully on behalf of us all.

Conclusions

1. The poet of this psalm worships Yahweh, the "faithful Creator" (1 Peter 4:19).
2. This hymn may have been sung on special occasions, such as at the New Year Festival, but it filled a very necessary spot in the theology of all who were grateful for God's successful instruction in a grand ecology.
3. We ought to have a profound appreciation for the beauty of God's creation, but we are warned against communing with nature itself. Instead, true appreciation for a proper ecology rests in a worship and exaltation of the Creator and not the creation itself.

Study Questions And Discussion Starters

1. In what order has the psalmist chosen to present the seven works of God in creation? Does this mean it is a mere copy of Genesis, or does it have additional striking features to add that the older form did not have?
2. Despite some trivial points of contact between the Egyptian "Hymn to Aton" (the Egyptian sun god), what are the main differences between this hymn and Psalm 104? How do these differences sharpen the meaning and argument for God alone being the Creator of the cosmos?
3. Discuss how God is said to be invisible, yet he "wraps (or clothes) himself in light" (v. 2)? Furthermore, if God is spirit (John 4:24), why does this psalm depict the beams of God's abode in heaven as if things were physical there (v. 3)?

4. If the "deep" forming the oceans covers three-fourths of the earth, how did God limit the extent of these oceans (vv. 8–11)? What does this demonstrate about creation?

5. As the psalmist takes time to pause in verse 24, what points does he make about the extent and the quality of God's creation? How do verses 31–35 reinforce that idea by noting what happens even from the personal touch of the maker of heaven and earth on the mountains? (Note 1 Peter 4:19 and its use of the title "the faithful Creator.")

6. What is present in God's work in creation that was climactically necessary when he made beasts to differ from humanity (v. 30)? How does God continue to provide for all these creatures (vv. 27–29)?

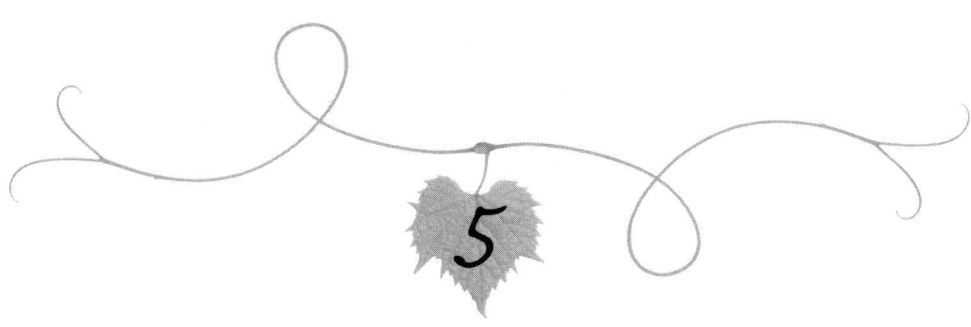

How Magnificent Is God's Name in All the Earth

PSALMS 8 AND 19:1–6

Walter C. Kaiser Jr.

Milton Lichtman died at the age of eighty-seven. Though his name may not ring a bell, chances are that anyone who has watched TV at any point in the past thirty years or so has seen him. An actor using the name Jan Leighton, he played 2,407 different roles over the course of his career. Hence his obituary said that Mr. Leighton was both *ubiquitous* and *anonymous*. The actor who played everyone!

Apart from movies and TV dramas, Lichtman's primary claim to fame was dressing up as historical figures—more than four hundred of them—and appearing in TV commercials. We're told that in disguise, Mr. Leighton lit a cigar as Fidel Castro in a commercial for lighters, sold cars as Albert Einstein for a Southern California car dealership, promoted a Minnesota savings bank as Abraham Lincoln, and touted an Arizona department store as Robert E. Lee. For one bank commercial he portrayed Clark Gable, Groucho Marx, Teddy Roosevelt, and Franklin Delano Roosevelt, all complaining about other banks that charged for checks.

He pitched cereal as Alexander Hamilton, beer as Johann Sebastian Bach, early mobile phones as Dracula, and cough syrup as Frankenstein. Among others, Vince Lombardi, Babe Ruth, Gandhi, Mozart, Charlie Chan, Sherlock Holmes, Ebenezer Scrooge, Humphrey Bogart, John Wayne, Thomas Jefferson, Ernest Hemingway, Charlemagne, Darwin, Wyatt Earp, Walter Cronkite, and even Margaret Thatcher were in his repertoire.

The glorious anonymity of his work was something Mr. Leighton embraced. Asked once how he was doing, he replied, "I'm alive and well and living in someone else's face."[1]

Reading this means that you are alive and living in your own face, so to speak, and being yourself! Meaning, since you were created in the image of God you possess a certain intentional, God-given, God-defined, God-derived glory. You don't have to create it, rush off to find it, or take on a persona. Even still, there is one key matter you are summoned to do by virtue of who you are as a human being. It is not a role, or a temporary bit part. It is integral to who you are. Namely, we are created and called to make Yahweh the center and object of our praise. This brings us to Psalms 8 and 19:1–6.

It is not difficult to recognize the hymnic quality of Psalm 8, for it weaves together a number of elements in a poetic blend that rises to high praise of our God. But more than this, Psalms 8 and 19:1–6, along with Psalms 29, 33, and 145, must be classified as "Songs of Creation."

Psalm 8 also is a good example of the figure of speech known as *inclusion*, for it begins in verse 1 with the words:

O Yahweh, our Sovereign,
How magnificent is your name
    in the whole of the earth. (translation mine)

And that is exactly how the psalm ends in verse 9, for it uses the very same words to close the psalm. Therefore, this is a psalm that praises Yahweh not only for making the world, but also, as it also turns out, for making it for the sake of the man on whom he has conferred the honor and the responsibility of being its steward and keeper. Instead of making man the center of praise, then, this psalm clearly makes Yahweh the center and object of the praise of all mortals (vv. 1, 9).

In the psalm's praise of the Lord, however, the psalmist in this portion of the Hebrew Scriptures did not follow the path of other Near Eastern countries, which typically expressed joy and delight in the world of nature and things themselves without linking it with the Creator. This view is called *pantheism,* because it deifies and glorifies nature and the world

---

[1] Bruce Webber, "Jan Leighton, Actor Who Played Everyone, Dies at 87," *New York Times,* November 28, 2009, accessed November 30, 2009, http://www.nytimes.com/2009/11/28/theater/28leighton.html?_r=0.

itself apart from any concept of a Creator God who made it all. Biblical theism, however, refuses to break and to separate nature as an entirely distinct entity apart from the divine maker of heaven and earth. On the contrary, biblical theism continues to be grateful for all that nature provides, but it places its top emphasis on God himself as the good Creator, ruler, and sustainer of it all.

Focal Point:	vv. 1, 9 "O Lord, our Lord, how majestic is your name in all the earth! You have set your glory above the heavens."
Homiletical Keyword:	Praises
Interrogative:	What? (What are the praises that are lifted up to our Lord for his work in creation?)

I.   PRELUDE: GLORY AND PRAISE TO OUR GOD FOR HIS CREATION (Ps. 8:1)

II. ENCOMIUM: PRAISE TO OUR GOD FOR HIS CREATION OF THE MOON AND THE STARS (Ps. 8:2–3)

III. ENCOMIUM: PRAISE TO OUR GOD FOR HIS CREATION OF MAN (Ps. 8:4–8)

IV. POSTLUDE: PRAISE TO OUR GOD FOR HIS CREATION (Ps. 8:9)

―――――――――――――――――――――――

I.   PRELUDE: GLORY AND PRAISE TO OUR GOD FOR HIS CREATION (Ps. 8:1)

It is nearly impossible to describe the greatness of our God in language that is adequate and suitable to match who he is and what he has done! Yet the Hebrew songs of praises are never merely descriptive.

Instead they attempt to draw pictures of what they are trying to say, without focusing merely on the picture for its own sake.

One can, therefore, almost imagine David on one of those frequent occasions, where he was alone by himself out in the quiet countryside tending his sheep, as he lay on the hillside gazing up at the night skies of the moon and the stars. In that open sky of the Near East, the stars would have appeared in all their brilliance as a display of the glory of God and the majesty of his name and works in creation.

The glory of God, sang David, exceeds the heights of the heavens with the planets and the stars giving him, and we who have now come after David, only a partial view of how great our God really is! Nevertheless, we ask how is it possible, then, for some educated and sophisticated mortals to shrug off this magnificent pageantry, and all the other evidence for the power and magnificence of God, as if it did not exist, or even often boggled our minds in all of its splendor? On the contrary, the heavens surely do declare the glory of God for any and all who will dare to take time to reflect on such a magnificent world!

II.   ENCOMIUM: PRAISE TO OUR GOD FOR HIS CREATION OF THE
      MOON AND THE STARS (PS. 8:2–3)

Hebrew mothers often did not wean their children until they were two or three years old. Thus, the children singled out here were young indeed, for some were still at the suckling stage. Moreover, whether we understand this to mean babies in a literal way, or we take it as meaning those who are disciples of the Lord, it is still a fact that from this group God has formed a bulwark against all opposing foes. The point is a strong one, for God has established his power on what others would regard as the weakest source of his help. Thus, despite the age in life, or the maturity in the gospel, from these newborn persons, God has mounted his best line of defense and strength.

When the psalmists and all mortals look at the heavens, which are here called in a wonderful figure of speech, "the work of [God's] fingers," we enter into the benefits and the study of astronomy, which, as few other studies do, proclaims God's greatness and our own insignificance. In the sphere of the heavens, distances must be measured in terms of light-years, that is, the distance light travels in one whole year at the speed of 186,000 miles per second.

Light does travel at that same constant speed of 186,000 miles per second, meaning that light from these stars can travel at the mind-boggling rate of something around six trillion miles in just one year! However, to impress our modern minds even more, we now know that some stars are billions of light-years from the earth. No wonder, then, that the psalmist gazing into the heavens, even with the limited understanding of the times he lived in, made his mind soar to unexpected heights of the knowledge and joy of such contemplations, while trying to imagine how great his God was in his person as judged from some of the works of his hands!

It was God who set the moon and the stars in place! That should be the number one thought in the minds of all mortals to help us see where we fit into the universe and its plans. But what an enormous space has God created for the expansive universe, consisting of all the planets and stars! If we have trouble trying to capture the enormity of the universe, how will we ever be able to begin to capture the enormity and immensity of our Lord in his person? But David surely sees the heavens as witnessing to the greatness of our God in a way that will certainly lead to praising him for all his works.

III. Encomium: Praise to Our God for His Creation of Man
     (Ps. 8:4–8)

When thought of against the backdrop of the immensity of the heavens, the first feeling one immediately gets is one of an overpowering sense of all mortals' insignificance in comparison to the universe, let alone to God himself! It is not only the mysterious depth and unrivaled glory that the heavens raise in our minds, but the comparison with what we see in the life of all mortals on this earth. How exceedingly small must humanity seem in the eyes of the Creator, who has made so many more, so much larger, and so much more spectacular things in the heavens, than what we mortals appear to be by ourselves. In fact, the Hebrew word for "man" (Hebrew 'enosh), is one of three key terms for man, but this one denotes man's weakness and fragility, recalling even the very memory of our origins from the dust of the earth.

But the good news is that through God's marvelous condescension, God has made this first man (and all who followed him) great by giving to him a status that is a little less than what is divine in nature, and he has also made him lord over all creation! Moreover, the reference in verse 6 to our Lord having "made [man] ruler over the works of [his] hands" is a clear reference to Genesis 1:26, with an allusion to the fact that God has made men and women in his very own image!

When we turn to the New Testament, however, these verses are twice applied to Christ himself in 1 Corinthians 15:27 and Hebrews 2:6–9, with the only change being the use of the third-person instead of the second-person pronoun used in Psalm 8. Thus, the complete subjugation of the whole universe to Christ is highlighted in these New Testament texts. The words of the psalm, however, are true of mortal man as well, even though these words have their highest sense in Christ, who is the head of all humanity. It is as Calvin has said, that so far as the human nature of Christ is concerned, all that has been freely bestowed on mortal man is heightened and more wonderfully reflected in the Son of Man, Jesus Christ. While the quotation in Hebrews 2:7 reflects not the greatness but the humiliation of man, the writer of Hebrews was not trying to interpret this text from Psalm 8 at this point for its meaning, or the basis for his authority, for he turned the words and used them instead for his own purposes, so that now the words took on a different sense. In other words, the New Testament writer appropriated and borrowed the words to express a new thought, one that was all his own and that is only found in the new context.

Nevertheless, the writer does not entirely set aside this reference to man in the psalm, for he does admit and base that part of his argument on that aspect of the psalm that speaks directly of mortal man. To be sure, he also tells us of the great things God has done in making man and giving to him honor and tasks. God has put a crown on his head, a scepter in his hand, and he has made him a little lower than God in the area of glory and power.

But there is another caveat in this whole work of doing so much for humanity, for all of this divine calling that God originally gave to mortals has never been fulfilled by men and women to the degree God intended for them. Thus, the great purpose of creation remains to be fulfilled. However, thanks be to God, there is One Perfect Man, who has stooped to take on our human nature, and then was raised in that nature to a lordship over all creation. That is our Lord Jesus.

In God's plan, man was meant to be a king, for he had a crown put on his head (v. 5b), and he was given a territory and subjects in the flocks, herds, beasts of the field, birds in the sky, and fish that swim in the paths of the sea (vv. 6–8). This is an extremely extensive realm for such a dominion. Thanks be to God for all his works!

IV.   POSTLUDE: PRAISE TO OUR GOD FOR HIS CREATION (PS. 8:9)

The psalm closes with the same words of appreciation and laudatory praise that it began with in verse 1. Its repetition here has the same effect as the repetition of a line in music, for the same words repeated over again can now do more than merely touch the ear and mind. Now these same words have an opportunity to touch the heart as well. Surely, it is true: "How majestic is [God's] name in all the earth!"

Now we turn to another psalm that speaks of God's majesty in creation, namely, Psalm 19:1–6.

It would seem that our minds are on the verge of exploding from what we have learned from Psalm 8, but Psalm 19:1–6 calls us to listen once again to what the heavens are telling us about the glory of God. The heavens are spectacular beyond our imagination. For example, the light from its stars and galaxies travels, as we have already noted, at 186,000 miles per second, which would mean that in one year, that distant light from any given star has covered some six trillion miles to enter our viewing point, yet that has been going on umpteen numbers of years! The reality of these light-years continues to boggle our minds and stir our hearts to praise God.

Some astronomers believe that the universe has no boundaries or edges as we might imagine it. But if we were able to ride at the speed of light, 186,000 miles per second, to reach the farthest point we can see on the present reach of our telescopes, it would take us ten billion years of travel to reach that point! Moreover, we can only see with the naked eye some five thousand stars, and with a small telescope some two million stars, or even with a large telescope such as the Palomar telescope, we can see billions of galaxies, not to mention a multitude of stars in those galaxies. Yet this is only the beginning of the wonders God has made. Truly, the heavens are telling the glory of God!

Focal Point:	v. 1 "The heavens declare the glory of God; the skies proclaim the work of his hands."
Homiletical Keyword:	Proclamations
Interrogative:	What? (What are the proclamations that the heavens make about the glory of God?)

I.   THE WORK OF GOD'S HANDS AS PROCLAIMED BY THE HEAVENS AND THE SKIES (PS. 19:1)

II. THE CONTINUAL SPEECH THE HEAVENS PROCLAIM (PS. 19:2–4A)

III. THE SUN AS A CHIEF HERALD OF GOD'S PRAISE (PS. 19:4B–6)

I.   THE WORK OF GOD'S HANDS AS PROCLAIMED BY THE HEAVENS AND THE SKIES (PS. 19:1)

The psalmist begins this psalm with the impression that the magnificence of God's creation has made on him and on all who will pause to examine God's handiwork. First, the fact of the heaven's declaration is asserted in verse 1a, which is followed by a statement of just how this was done: it was by their bearing witness to the fact that God made them.

The real source of the splendor and pomp of the heavens that fills the skies with the beauty that is so attractive to the eye is God the Creator, and not chance or such related ideas. It is our Lord who created them and they were made to show forth his glory. God's hands and fingers, to speak for the moment in a figurative way, fashioned the stars and planets. It was he who clothed them with light as if that light were their garments, while placing the sun in the midst of them, in our own galaxy, to radiate his praise.

II.   The Continual Speech the Heavens Proclaim (Ps. 19:2–4a)

Verse 2 continues the personification by noting that "day after day" and "night after night," this testimony has continued to speak on behalf of the Creator's spectacular work! There is no letup or interruption in the continual message the heavens proclaim about the majesty and magnificence of the creation of God. It is as if the stars and planets all had a speech of their own with a clear message that pointed consistently to their Creator, our Lord.

To be sure, verse 3 qualifies the speech that is sent forth as a message that is "inaudible" ("not heard"), but this language is not a type of discourse that may be classified with the known dialects on earth. In fact, these astral bodies have a voice, but it is one that addresses the understanding heart rather than the ear or the mind.

This testimony to the greatness of God's creation in the heavens is so replete with a message, brimming over with truth for all who will listen with an understanding heart that the compass and extent of its message have gone out to the whole earth. The words these heavenly bodies proclaim have now reached, as it continues to extend outward, to the ends of the earth. Therefore, God has not left himself without a witness throughout the whole world, for the sky keeps shining forth a message that is meant to capture the heart of every mortal on planet earth in confronting the fact that there is a maker of heaven and earth.

The apostle Paul asked this very same question in Romans 10:18 when he posed the question, "Did they [i.e., the nations at large] not hear?" "Of course they did," Paul retorted, for he went on to cite as his proof our verse from Psalm 19:4: "Their voice has gone out into all the earth, their words to the ends of the world." Paul had just announced that "faith comes from hearing the message, and the message is heard through the word about Christ" (Rom. 10:17). Thus, the message of God's revelation in nature is as extensive in its reach as is the verbal message of the gospel! It is not necessary to import an allegorical meaning to this part of the psalm, as some of the older interpreters, including Luther, have done. In Luther's strange allegorical reading of the psalm, as he quoted Romans 10:18, the heavens are made a figure of the church, and the sun is made a figure of the gospel. But the literal meaning will suit the passage and the apostle much better.

The fabric of the world exhibits a beautiful order in its arrangement and in its manifestation of the perfections God has built into all its correlations. In the face of so much beauty and so much perfection, it seems more than just a trivial response to attribute all of this to mere chance or accident. There is too much wisdom evident in its conception, planning, and orderly movement to conclude that it was anything but an intentional act of God!

III. THE SUN AS A CHIEF HERALD OF GOD'S PRAISE (PS. 19:4B–6)

Life on earth without the sun would be dreadful! But God has set not only the sun but also a tent or a pavilion in the heavens for the sun, which is how the psalmist portrays the rising of the sun each day. Moreover, the sun is metaphorically compared to a bridegroom and a champion (v. 5), who joyously goes forth from his wedding canopy, the bridal chamber, with the same radiance as the sun goes forth daily from its tent or pavilion. As a champion (or valiant man), the sun rejoices to run its course (v. 5). Indeed, the sun rises at one end of the heavens and makes its circuit to the other; nothing is hidden from its heat (v. 6). Life on earth depends on the regularity of the sun, but that regularity has come from the order imposed on it by the sun's Creator.

The power, radiance, and reliability of the sun reveal the glory of God, as well as his wisdom and perfection. Once again, there are no words to be heard, but the effect of the sun is all too evident: "nothing is hidden from its heat" (v. 6b NASB). Consequently, as the morning light of the sun radiates in all its freshness and cheerfulness, so mortals are led to give thanks to God for all the beauty and splendor seen in the work God has completed in the heavens.

CONCLUSIONS

1. There is a constant but beautiful message from the heavens that bears witness to the work of the Creator as seen from their witness to the Lord.
2. This message is so strong that it has gone out over the whole earth.

3.   Our God has not left himself without a witness, which should arrest the attention of all mortals in all nations to move from the clear indications of his work in creation and the physical order of things to learn of his work in redemption for us as well.

Study Questions and Discussion Starters

1.   Can you name at least five psalms that celebrate God's work in creation or that can be classified as possible "Songs of Creation"?
2.   What is the name of the philosophy that deifies and glories in nature itself apart from expressing our joy and delight in the Creator who made all these wonderful things? Contrast that with biblical theism.
3.   Discuss what experiences you have had as you have contemplated the work of God in forming the heavens that are so immense that light traveling at 186,000 miles per second, or some 6,000,000,000,000 (six trillion) miles in a year, has traveled such a great distance to be seen by us (8:3; 19:1–2)! If we were to travel at this rate of speed today, how many years would it take us to get to what some regard as the edge of the universe (19:1)?
4.   Even though the heavens appear to be more spectacular because of their immensity, what distinctive honors has God given to humans, and in what sort of eminence does such a human being sit with regard to the rest of creation (8:5–6)? How was this message from the psalmist used in the New Testament, and what was being taught there?
5.   How extensive and how powerful is the message about the greatness of God's creation (19:3–4)? Compare Paul's use of this text in Romans 10:17–18.
6.   Discuss why the sun (19:4b–6) is compared to a bridegroom, or a champion who goes forth from his *huppah,* the Jewish bridal chamber, to make its circuit of the earth every day.

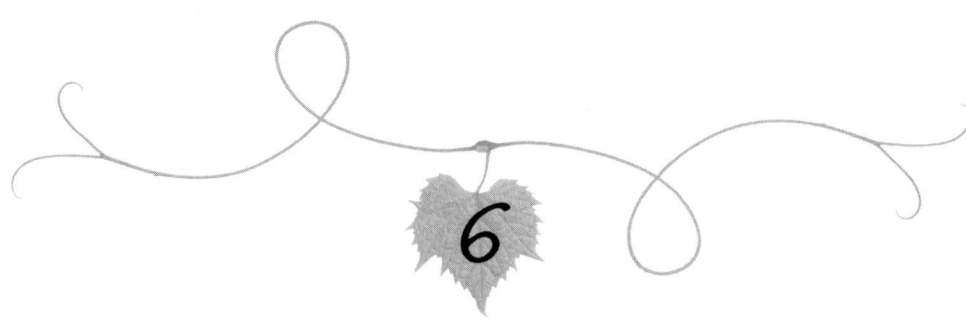

6

THE LORD OF THE SEVEN THUNDERS

PSALM 29

Walter C. Kaiser Jr.

The approach of the thunderstorm in Psalm 29 reminds me of my years growing up in farmhouse outside of Philadelphia. Our farm was the very last house at the end of the electric line for that area, but the electric company had failed to ground this line into the earth until some years later. Invariably, when a summer thunderstorm would occur, my mother would call the four of us boys and two girls (I was the oldest) to come quickly into the farmhouse and wait out the storm indoors. However, occasionally the lightning would hit the power lines to our house and the lightning would travel down the power lines to our basement. It would then crack in our cellar and arc across our living room from the sockets in the baseboards around the room. That meant we sat on the sofa and chairs with our legs up off the floor to avoid any shocking experiences. I grew up, then, with a high regard for thunderstorms!

Psalm 29 treats a thunderstorm perhaps like the ones I remember from my childhood. Even though only two poems in the book of the Psalter carry the title "Psalm of Praise" within their hymn to the Lord of nature, namely, Psalms 100 and 145, the whole book of hymns is called in Hebrew *Tehillim,* "Praises." But if this is so, then why does the book of Psalms, which is so filled with prayers, laments, and confessions, have as its overall title "Praises"?

The answer seems to lie in the fact that all the prayers, laments, and confessions come in the context of public worship at the tabernacle or temple. Therefore, mortals reached their highest level of biblical worship when they placed their obsession with sin and the resulting guilt along with their personal needs in the hands of their Creator, Judge, and Savior. As they responded with gratefulness to the one who was himself the grace of life, who could sustain them in each and every distress of life, what flowed forth from their mouths was embraced in the name of "Praises," a title that shows that in the act of adoration, each mortal is able to rise above all their various personal moods and attitudes.

But there also are a number of Psalms that can be classified in the strictest sense as a type of "hymn of praise." In these psalms, the poet steps aside so that he may adore his God rather than focus on his own feelings of guilt, need, or confession. Generally, this involves one of three great themes in Scripture: (1) celebrating God as sovereign over nature, (2) celebrating God as ruler of history, and (3) celebrating God as Lord of Zion. Psalm 29 is of this first type, for it exalts in God as sovereign over nature itself as he speaks through the thunder of the storm.

Moreover, in the case of Psalm 29, it is the psalmist's joy of contemplating the work of God both in creation and in providence that becomes the focus of his joy and praise to God. Such manifestations of God's hand in the world of material things can be seen both in ordinary times and in the face of the terrors of one of those thunderstorms in the Near East, which were so awesome in their power and their force. So whether the meditation on the works of God be in the quiet hours of the day or night (Pss. 8, 19), or in contemplation of the whole range of God's works in the cosmos (Ps. 104), the psalmists never depict nature as something that is benign, or not worthy of singing forth the praises to God for all he is and has done. It is in that light that we too look at Psalm 29 in order to learn how to praise our great Creator and Lord of the universe! It will also give us a peek into what God did in creating the universe.

Focal Point:	v. 3
	"The voice of the Lord is over the waters; the God of glory thunders, the Lord thunders over the mighty waters."
Homiletical Keyword:	Awakenings

Interrogative:	What?
	(What are the awakenings
	the 29th psalm stirs within
	us to offer praise to God
	for his marvelous works
	in creation?)

I.   PRELUDE: PRAISING GOD FOR HIS THUNDERING VOICE (Ps. 29:1–2)

II.   THE GATHERING: PRAISING GOD FOR HIS CREATIVE ACTS IN
      NATURE WITH THE ACT OF WORSHIP IN THE TEMPLE (Ps. 29:3–4)

III. THE BURSTING FORTH: ADORING GOD AT THE MOMENT THE
      STORM FROM THE SEA HITS THE LAND (Ps. 29:5–7)

IV.   THE QUIETUDE: GIVING THANKS TO GOD FOR THE TEMPEST'S
      SWIFT PASSING TO THE WILDERNESS (Ps. 29:8–9)

V.   THE POSTLUDE: MEDITATING ON THE AFTER-CALM AS YAHWEH
      HAS KEPT THE STORM WITHIN HIS BOUNDS (Ps. 29:10–11)

I.   PRELUDE: PRAISING GOD FOR HIS THUNDERING VOICE
      (Ps. 29:1–2)

Franz Delitzsch called this hymn "the Psalm of the Seven Thunders," because the Hebrew expression *qol Yahweh,* "voice of the Lord," occurs seven times in this hymn as the theme unfolds (compare to the Canaanite Ugaritic *ql,* "voice"). Thus, centuries later, the New Testament book of Revelation 10:3 probably alluded to this same expression as the mighty angel of God did when he spoke: "And he gave a loud shout like the roar of a lion. When he shouted, the voices of the seven thunders spoke."

In the Canaanite literature the pagan god Baal is said to give voice in the form of thunder, for he was known as the storm god. But most of all, the imagery in Psalm 29 describes a mighty storm that typically formed over the Mediterranean Sea and then swept inland across the magnificent forested mountains of Lebanon in the north before quietly leaving as it ended up south in the desert of Kadesh.

This psalm begins with a prelude of a threefold call to adoration, perhaps sung antiphonally by three different choirs as they converge on the sanctuary's esplanade. The triple repetition of the first call to "Ascribe to the Lord" makes this invitation all the more pressing and forceful. By this we too are urged to raise our voices in praise in the presence of the majesty of our Creator!

As already noted, recent studies have suggested that the literary origins of the genre of this poem may have begun in the archaic liturgy from the ancient alphabetic Ugaritic script in Phoenicia (ca. 1200–1400 BC). This may be reflected in the fact that the invitation is issued directly to "the sons of the gods/O mighty ones" (v. 1a, my translation), but the control of the world was most assuredly still in the hands of the omnipotent one, Yahweh himself. As used here, the "sons of gods" do not represent pagan idols or deities, as some assume, but members of the divine court, as seen also in Job 1–3. These were supernatural beings (perhaps angels) that inhabit the heavenly realms. Note in Psalm 89:5–7, the same Hebrew expression is translated by the NIV as "heavenly beings" and is found in poetic parallelism with "the assembly of the holy ones," whose task seems to be to praise Yahweh in the heavenly realm. Therefore, if that is the response of heaven, our response as earthly benefactors ought to be no less, since we are the principal users of all God has made.

The verb translated as "ascribe" (or "give") (Hebrew *habu*) is somewhat unusual, for it is a cognate of the noun "love" (Hebrew *'ahab*). Accordingly, from the very first word in this psalm, we have a commentary on what is the real nature of biblical worship. The members of the divine court in heaven are bidden to "ascribe lovingly" both "glory and power" to Yahweh for all his mighty works in creation and providence. They too must submit themselves to the one and only powerful God as they too render unto him the "glory due his name" (v. 2a) and "worship the Lord in the splendor of his holiness" (v. 2b).

The God whom we must all worship is the one who manifests his glory in such a supreme fashion that it discloses his name in all of its characteristics, power, and qualities.

Thus a threefold call has been issued not only for the heavenly beings but also, by implication, to all those who are distinguished and not as well known on earth. Three great reasons are given for such an exuberant celebration: (1) all beings, both in heaven and on earth, are called to recognize the distinctive work of God in the world he has made; (2) they are also called to give special thanks to God for revealing his name as he communicates by that name to all mortals his will, his plan, and his intentions for his people; and (3) they are called to "worship (or prostrate themselves) in the face of the beauty of his holiness" (my translation).

II.   THE GATHERING: PRAISING GOD FOR HIS CREATIVE ACTS IN NATURE WITH THE ACT OF WORSHIP IN THE TEMPLE (PS. 29:3–4)

Everything in this psalm fits the pattern of a typical electrical storm with thunder and lightning that appear so frequently in the rainy season of Palestine. As the first of the three middle strophes of this psalm begins, we hear the rumblings of the storm coming in from the western horizon of the Mediterranean Sea. Here, these peals of thunder are likened to the voice of the Lord. Their sound intensifies over the watery sea but then explodes powerfully as it approaches (v. 4a) and as the storm draws near.

There is a majesty in an electrical thunderstorm, most will agree, for all of nature is called on to pause as it awaits the onrush of the rainfall that will certainly follow the loud booms of thunder in the clouds. It is not in passing that the sea was often used as the image of the epitome of chaotic forces, even in the Baal myths from Canaan, but the waters of the sea posed no such problem for Yahweh. He was Lord over the waters, so how could any of the waters or the sea be a source of fear and terror?

But it must not be forgotten that the "voice" (or "sound") was here depicting the majesty of the voice of God. God was not to be worshiped and praised for his acts in creation alone, for along with those great creations he had also spoken so that mortals could get an understanding for what was going on and what would happen in the future by revealing his name and nature along with those acts. His voice alone was enough to help mortals sense the splendor and majesty of his divine being and what all of this meant!

III.   THE BURSTING FORTH: ADORING GOD AT THE MOMENT THE STORM FROM THE SEA HITS THE LAND (PS. 29:5–7)

The thunder, which in this case was the triumphant voice of the Lord, moved with the storm from out in the Mediterranean Sea and came crashing in onto land in Phoenicia (Lebanon). At first it hit the coastal range of Phoenicia, where the fabled cedar trees grew, but even those trees, that were so famous a source in the ancient world for providing the best source of the stoutest timber available for construction, was splintered by the bolts of lightning that hit and felled some of those same trees (v. 5). It was a matter of record that the kings from Egypt to Mesopotamia routinely marched to Lebanon for this cedar lumber, as Kings David and Solomon negotiated for this lumber in the building of their palaces and Yahweh's temple (2 Sam. 5:11; 1 Kings 5:6–9). Thus, the cedars of Lebanon, symbols of such dependable solidarity, are both broken (v. 5a) and shattered to pieces (v. 5b) by some of the lightning bolts announced by the thunder. So much for what was thought to be the most solid and enduring material aspects of our world against the mighty voice of God. It simply could not stand up to the splendor of God's power and might!

The lightning was accompanied by "strikes" (v. 7), for God often used his lightning bolts as one of his weapons. Therefore, Yahweh could, if needed, strike with the power of lightning. Was this not enough of a reason for all the earth to sit up and take notice of the voice of God?

What was taking place on the Lebanon range in this storm was simultaneously happening on the snowy, towering peak of Mount Hermon (9,232 feet high), here called "Sirion" (v. 6b; cf. Deut. 3:9). Sirion was one of the highest mountains in the vicinity of Israel. But even these mighty mountain ranges shook and quaked when God spoke, for they were likened to powerful young bulls and oxen skipping about (cf. Ps. 114:4). What appeared so solid and immoveable was being tossed about as if it were nothing at all in the face of God's power and majesty. Thus, on this identification, the storm tracked down to south of Judea to Kadesh. However, there is another possible location for "the wilderness of Kadesh," and that is the region near Qadesh, north of Damascus on the Orontes River. It is difficult to say which site was intended in this psalm, but we assume it must be the southern location because of its use in Israel's psalter.

IV. The Quietude: Giving Thanks to God for the Tempest's
     Swift Passing to the Wilderness (Ps. 29:8–9)

As the crescendo of the first two strokes of this middle section die down, there is a stirring in the desert as the tempest quickly flees from the north to the south, and then fades into nonexistence in the wilderness of Kadesh. It is as if nature finally pauses in a wounded and exhausted way from the magnitude of the storm. But this is sharply to be contrasted with what is being said in the temple: "Glory [to God]" (v. 9c), all of which spoke of the awesome presence and outsplashing of the sheer fact that God was there in all his mighty presence and power!

Here, then, is the response to the appeal of the prelude. All are agreed: the supernatural beings in heaven along with the mortals on earth shout "glory and praise" to the Lord of the storm. But he is our Lord who has communicated with us in his word; a word that should cause us to bow in respect and awe of his person and work!

V.   THE POSTLUDE: MEDITATING ON THE AFTER-CALM AS YAHWEH HAS KEPT THE STORM WITHIN HIS BOUNDS (Ps. 29:10–11)

The storm is now over and passed. So the psalmist returns to the scene in the heavenly court (v. 10) where "Yahweh sits enthroned over the flood" (v. 10a, my translation). The word "flood" is used elsewhere only when referring to the great flood in the time of Noah (Gen. 6:17; 7:10). Yahweh's power clearly is higher and stronger than the "mighty waters" (Ps. 29:3), or the sea itself, as is his sovereignty over the highest of all potentates in the world of that day or this. That is why Yahweh is "King forever" (v. 10b).

Moreover, the Lord gives "strength to his people" (v. 11a) and he "blesses his people with peace" (v. 11b). His prayer is that the power seen in the making and sustaining of all things from his creative hand may also be, in part, endued to his people as they clearly hear the thunder of his voice and obey him wholeheartedly.

CONCLUSIONS

1. Even in the face of the terrors of a violent thunderstorm, there is complete trust in the securing and protecting hand of God.
2. The manifold displays of the hand of the Creator who gave life itself should be enough to cause to well up within us thoughts of the glory and power that must now be ascribed to the name of our God.

3. God's voice is so clear; it is like the thunder of an electrical storm, for his work cannot be quenched or set aside as being unimportant.

4. At the end of the storm, Yahweh still sits enthroned over the flood and over the kingdoms of men, for he gives power to his people and blesses them with peace. Therefore, let us exalt his name and give thanks for all his creation and for what he has accomplished on our behalf.

Study Questions and Discussion Starters

1. Why is the book of Psalms called, in Hebrew, the book of "Praises" when it is filled with so many prayers, laments, and confessions?

2. Why is Psalm 29 called "The Psalm of the Seven Thunders," and how is that title reminiscent of some of the Canaanite Ugaritic literature? How does this title of our study anticipate Revelation 10:3?

3. How does this psalm fit the pattern and progress of a typical electrical storm in the Near East? What has been your experience with a thunderstorm?

4. Who are the "mighty ones" (v. 1), or as others translate this expression, the "the sons of the gods/mighty ones"? Does this expression occur elsewhere in Psalms, and if so, what are the tasks and possible identities of those so called?

5. Why does David introduce the "flood" of Noah in verse 10, and how does that elevate the type of rejoicing and praise to God in this psalm?

6. Discuss how the work of our Lord as Creator is enhanced by Psalm 29.

7. In what ways is the language of Psalm 29 counter to much of the secular discussions of origins in today's world?

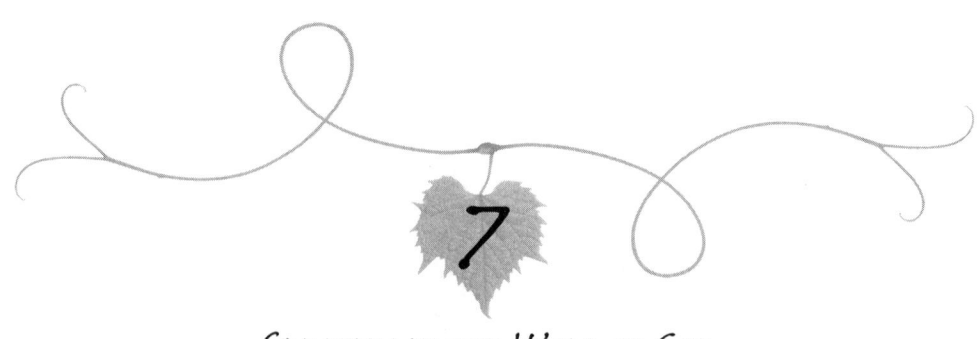

CREATION BY THE WORD OF GOD

PSALM 33:6–13

Walter C. Kaiser Jr.

Never underestimate the power of the spoken word. Masses have been moved by oration, both for good and for ill. History is replete with examples of those who have inspired others to their cause on the brink of battle, or at defining moments in the life of a nation directing its future by the force of the word. But as powerful as oratory is, it is not all-powerful. In fact, there is only one who is all-powerful and who by the power of his word brings into existence *ex nihilo*, "out of nothing". He is the Lord God Almighty. Psalm 33 speaks of the Lord and the power of his word.

Though some see this psalm as one totally given over to praising the Lord for his work in creation, others more accurately view the psalm as also rendering praise for God's activities in nature and in human history. For the psalm does begin with praise to Yahweh (vv. 1–3), then it goes on to list a number of his perfections (vv. 4–5), before it comes to describing how he did, in fact, create and form the world by the power of his spoken word (vv. 6–9). However, the psalm continues to show how Yahweh is an all-wise (vv. 10–11), all-seeing (vv. 13–15), and sovereign God who rules the nations (vv. 16–17). He is also celebrated in this psalm for his watch-care (v. 18), preservation (v. 19), and protection (v. 20) over all those who fear and trust in him (v. 21). The psalm ends with a brief request that this same love may also be upon all who have hoped in him (v. 22).

This is one of the few psalms that does not have an inscription at the top of it. But it is certainly a psalm that celebrates the power and effectiveness of the awesome power of the spoken word of God. This same theology was repeated in John 1:1–3, which states: "In the beginning was the Word, and the Word was with God, and the Word was God. He was with God in the beginning. Through him all things were made; without him nothing was made that has been made." What a statement! Christ so embodied the Word that he himself was that Word. Moreover, "all things [in heaven and earth] were made by him" so that "without him, nothing was made that has been made." There are few clearer ways of saying that Christ was the Creator, source, and maker of this whole universe and all that is in it!

No less distinctive, however, are the words found in Hebrews 11:3. The writer of that text affirms: "By faith we understand that the universe was formed at God's command, so that what is seen was not made out of what was visible." That certainly is putting the matter in a straightforward manner! Everything that is visible in the world was made out from what previously had been invisible or just plain nonexistent! How, then, could it have come into being? It could only have come into being by the word spoken by the Creator at the time of its beginning. This was God's answer to the *how* of creation! God created the world by speaking it into existence.

The words of Psalm 33:6–11 are of great significance and importance, then, if we are to properly regard how the universe came into being. They deserve to be looked at in detail. They accord with Psalm 104:1–9, which is included in chapter 4 of this book.

Focal Point:	v. 9 "For [God] spoke, and it came to be; he commanded, and it stood firm."
Homiletical Keyword:	Results
Interrogative:	What? (What were the results of our Lord's speaking his creative word?)

I.   THE STARRY HEAVENS WERE FORMED (Ps. 33:6)

II.   THE WATERS OF THE SEA WERE GATHERED TOGETHER (Ps. 33:7)

III.   THE PEOPLES OF THE EARTH FEARED THE LORD (Ps. 33:8)

IV.   THE CREATION CAME INTO BEING (Ps. 33:9)

V.   THE PLANS OF THE LORD STOOD COMPLETE (Ps. 33:10–13)

I.   THE STARRY HEAVENS WERE FORMED (Ps. 33:6)

It was "by the word of the Lord [that] the heavens were made" (v. 6a). This attributes a huge amount of power and creativity to our Lord. The celestial bodies did not arrive by some work of chance or happenstance; nor did they come about by an expenditure of some sort of natural selection, or by some sort of physical effort by anyone else. Instead, Yahweh spoke all things into existence by the word of his mouth.

In fact, the parallel expression to the word of his mouth is "the breath of his mouth" (v. 6b). The two expressions, "the word of his mouth" and "the breath of his mouth," show that God formed all that exists only by means of the utterance of his will, not by any other means of effort or work on nature's part, or by the work of chance. These parallel expressions remind us of the same dual forms that were expressed as God formed man in Genesis 2:7. Adam was not complete until God had breathed into Adam's lungs the breath of life; only then did he become alive.

Likewise, it was by the "word of the Lord" that "the heavens were made" (v. 6a). Elsewhere Scripture uses "the breath of his lips" (Isa. 11:4) to issue a sentence of judgment, but in this instance the use of the breath of God's mouth was the source of life and the created order of life.

The host of the heavens spans a mighty expanse. It seems almost limitless in its reach as we try to calculate the distance in terms of light traveling at 186,000 miles per second, year after year, to reach us at this time! And all of this God brought into being by the word of his mouth.

II.   THE WATERS OF THE SEA WERE GATHERED TOGETHER (Ps. 33:7)

It is noteworthy that the heavens and the sea, two of the most extensive and massive parts of creation known to man, are mentioned as the showpieces of God's almighty power and creativity. The oceans, which cover three-fourths of the earth's surface, were gathered up in a heap as our Lord called them into existence.

The imagery of a heap suggests the appearance of the waves of the sea, which may be an expression borrowed from Exodus 15:8: "By the blast of your nostrils the waters [of the Nile River] piled up"; and Joshua 3:16: "The water [of the Jordan River] stopped flowing. It piled up in a heap a great distance away." Some have suggested that the sea is shut up by its shores, just as the heaps of corn are shut up by walls of the granary (Isa. 17:11). Moreover, the parallelism of the next member of verse 7 repeats the idea, only in a different form: "He puts the deep in storehouses." But both expressions are meant to verify the original act of creation in Genesis 1 where the waters were "gathered up."

III. THE PEOPLES OF THE EARTH FEARED THE LORD (Ps. 33:8)

Since the Lord God is the Creator and Ruler over all things he has made and the one by whose power even the constellations were made and are now held in place, therefore all the peoples of the earth must fear this great king (cf. Amos 4:13; 5:8; 9:6). This includes all the people of all the nations, for the wisest response they can make is one of terror and dread to God's power in creation and in history. God has made everything in the whole universe, so why should the nations not bow in submission to the fact that he alone is Creator and Ruler over all?

IV. THE CREATION CAME INTO BEING (Ps. 33:9)

Verse 9 seems to be a result of listening to Genesis 1:3: "And God said, 'Let there be light.'" The universe was not the result of an accident; it all happened just as God had spoken it into existence! Whatever God said, that is what came into being. This he did by his power and wisdom. Moreover, the order observed in the world today is the result of the order he arranged and put into place. Accordingly, God's sovereignty is no cause for dread or concern; instead, it is a comfort to all who know him and love him.

Not only did all things have their origins and being in the word of God, but as a result of God's speaking, all things held fast and "stood firm" after he had spoken (v. 9). This speaks to the reliability of our Lord and how faithful he is to fulfill all that he said.

V.   THE PLANS OF THE LORD STOOD COMPLETE (Ps. 33:10–13)

Following the presentation of the power of God's word in bringing the creation into being, the psalmist goes on to describe how God has brought order into the world to counter the "order" of man: "The Lord foils the plans of the nations; he thwarts the purposes of the peoples" (v. 10). While God's counsels and thoughts last forever, those of the sons and daughters of men fail and do not have any lasting effect. But God's plans cannot be thwarted, for what he has purposed will succeed.

No wonder, then, that verse 12 teaches that "blessed is the nation whose God is the Lord." For this verse anticipates what is said more fully in verses 18–20 in the doctrine of God's special universal providence.

CONCLUSIONS

1.   The immensity and volume created in the heavens and the seas alone are mind-boggling indeed.
2.   The power of God's spoken word is first seen in the created order.
3.   The world came into being as a result of God's speaking it into existence.
4.   All the order seen in creation is a result of God's speaking it into that arrangement.

STUDY QUESTIONS AND DISCUSSION STARTERS

1.   What are the points made by John 1:1–3 and Hebrews 11:3 that parallel the teaching of Psalm 33:6–11?
2.   How, according to Psalm 33:6, did the heavens and celestial bodies come into being? How does that affect our contemporary interpretations of the method of creation?
3.   What is the parallel expression in verse 6 to the "word of his mouth"? How is that similar and yet different from a dual form God used as he created the man in Genesis 2:7?

4. What are the two most massive forms and extensive parts of the creation in Psalm 33? What is the significance of these two works of God?

5. What sort of response does verse 8 call for in light of God's power shown in his making of the constellations and currently holding them in place?

6. How does the psalmist argue for God's sovereignty and our comfort in verse 9?

7. Discuss how the hand of God in creation is contrasted with the hand of God as it is exercised over the nations (vv. 10–13).

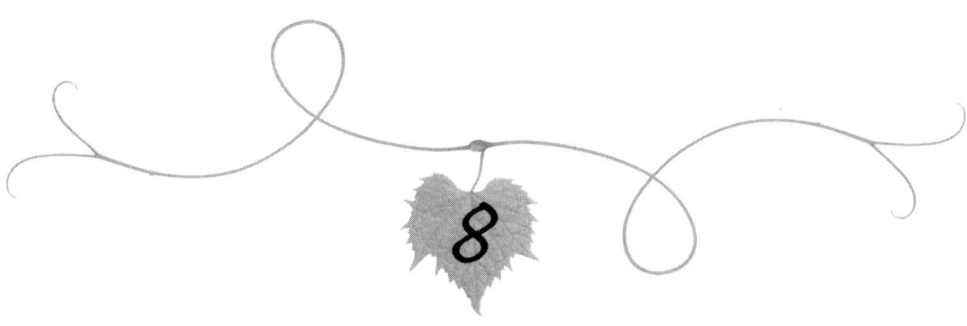

THE NOISE OF HEAVEN AND EARTH!

PSALM 148

Dorington G. Little

A debate rages about what the creation narrative of the opening chapters of Genesis actually teaches. Are the six days of creation literal days or geologic ages? Is the earth young or old? Is there room for theistic evolution? What about intelligent design? How does science fit in to all this? Does Genesis teach that God created out of nothing (*ex nihilo*) all that exists?

Is Genesis less (if anything) about the actual process of creation and simply or mainly about the sovereign reality of the Creator—his rule and reign as opposed to the so-called gods of the ancient Near East, who are really non-gods, a big fat nothing?

Not to minimize any of these views, or the importance of the debate as it ponders the connection between faith and science, Psalm 148 comes at this from an entirely different perspective.

Because it depicts a general correlation of the days of creation in Genesis 1, Psalm 148 is a response of the cosmos in its totality to the reality of its Creator. That is, the ultimate purpose of the Genesis creation narrative—as shown here by the psalmist—is praise! The cosmos, and the entirety therein, exists to praise God!

The way the psalmist sets this forth is to show the connection between *creation* and *praise* in verses 1–12 followed by the connection between *redemption* and *praise* in verses 13–14. This is because the pinnacle of creation is humanity, and the pinnacle of humanity is the redeemed people of God, as in new creation!

Focal Point:	vv. 1a and 14b "Praise the Lord!"
Homiletical Keyword:	Praise
Interrogative:	What? (What does the psalmist have to say about creation—its praise and redemption?)

I.   The Creation and Its Praise (Ps. 148:1–12)

II.   The Redeemed and Their Praise (Ps. 148:13–14)

I.   The Creation and Its Praise (Ps. 148:1–12)

Praising the Lord is a command and a summons, occurring over and over in the psalm—a command that applies to all that is. Praise the Lord from the heavens (v. 1) and praise the Lord from the earth (v. 7). Thus, verses 1–12 are arranged in two parts. The first six verses speak of the heavens and generally refer to the first two days of creation. Verses 7–12 speak of the earth and generally refer to days three through six of creation. This is not an exact commentary on each day of creation, but rather a theological reflection on creation and its ultimate purpose. "Heaven and earth" is the biblical way of speaking about all that exists. The nine occurrences of the word "all" is to ensure that we understand just how comprehensive this praise is!

All segments of creation—whether heavenly or earthly beings, inanimate or animate—exist to praise their Creator. As such, the Lord is to be praised from the heavens—in the heights, by the angels of God, by his mighty hosts who do his bidding and carry forth the Lord's rule.

Moreover, as the creation narrative unfolds, the expanse of the heavens in the sun, moon, and stars of light are all called to exuberantly pour forth in the expression of praise to the Lord: "Let them praise the name of the Lord!"[1] Why? "For He commanded and they were created. He has also established them forever and ever; He has made a decree which will not pass away" (vv. 5b–6).

In other words, the nature of their praise is by virtue of their existence and because God spoke them into existence, an existence ever dependent upon him. They praise because they exist in total dependence on God. That's why the stars are all the planetary luminaries of space. If you want to feel humbled, even minuscule, take a look at the recent, absolutely stunning, mind-boggling pictures beamed back to earth from the cameras on NASA's Cassini spacecraft. The spacecraft has been orbiting Saturn, the ringed planet, since 2004 and Saturn's rings are spectacularly in the foreground. The tiny pale blue dot of earth and our moon are 900 million miles away in the background in the sheer vastness of space.

One report called this an interplanetary paparazzo![2] And one scientist calls it an "interplanetary salute between robot and maker."[3] Yes, all true, yet the psalmist puts this salute in a different perspective. It is not just a salute between the product of human creativity and proud humans themselves. The objects of the heavens exist not for self-glorification and mutual interplanetary salute, but as a salute to God himself. A salute of praise! In Psalm 148 the planets are agents of praise, not objects of praise.

Certainly on one level, seeing such awe-inspiring pictures is completely humbling. Even more humbling is to see the earth in the wide-angle lens as just a distant speck—and then to think of our place in it and role on it. However, to ponder it with only that frame of reference is not fully accurate, since the psalmist reminds us that the purpose of the existence of distant planets and stars and suns is to praise God in their own humble dependence on God for all they are and will ever be!

---

[1] All biblical citations in my chapters (8, 10, and 12) are from the New American Standard Bible.

[2] David Freeman, "Cassini Earth Photos: Saturn Orbiter Snaps Amazing Images of Our Planet from 900 Million Miles Away," *The Huffington Post*, accessed May 6, 2014, http://www.huffingtonpost.com/2013/07/23/cassini-earth-photos-saturn-orbiter-images-planet_n_3637540.html?ir=Science.

[3] "NASA Releases Images of Earth Taken by Distant Spacecraft," Jet Propulsion Laboratory, NASA, accessed May 6, 2014, http://saturn.jpl.nasa.gov/news/newsreleases/newsrelease20130722/.

Bear in mind that the other nations of the ancient Near East idolized the sun, moon, and stars as actual deities, not simply as celestial orbs in their depth of field as they peered up into space on dark nights. So when the psalmist says these give praise to God, like Moses in Genesis, he is declaring that the supposed gods of the nations are subordinate to Yahweh. Indeed, there is only one true God—the God who created all that is. Therefore, all that is must praise him!

Resuming his command to praise (vv. 7–12), the psalmist focuses on the occupants and forces of earth, culminating in the pinnacle of creation, which is humanity itself. This includes everything . . .

. . . whether great and terrifying monsters emerging from the gloom of the deep sea

. . . whether forces of nature pelting the world with hail and snow

. . . whether stormy winds with rain-bearing clouds primed to deposit their deluge on parched land

. . . whether craggy 20,000-feet-high mountains or green rolling hills set among fertile plains with their crops laid out like patchwork

. . . whether wheat seemingly rolling like waves in the prairie wind, or apple trees blossoming and bearing Red Delicious, or cedar trees gnarled and standing tall even after 1,000 years

. . . whether tigers prowling dense and dark Sumatran jungles or Jersey dairy cattle grazing in the verdant fields of Vermont under blue skies

. . . whether the one-ton twenty-one-foot-long saltwater crocodile swimming the seas and stalking the coasts, rivers, and water holes of northern Australia

. . . or whether the three-inch-long, two-tenths of an ounce, ruby-throated green-feathered hummingbird acrobatically flitting through your backyard here in Massachusetts.

All these, just like the expanse of the cosmos, by virtue of their existence and dependence upon the Creator, are equally called to praise him. And of course, the pinnacle of creation—humanity—what are we called to do? The same! To praise God. To this end, notice how verses 11–12 unfold:

Kings of the earth and all peoples; princes and all judges of the earth;
both young men and virgins; old men and children.

Who receives the praise in our world? Who receives all the attention? It's those who are on the top of the heap, those who rule, those who govern, whether they be kings, princes, presidents, prime ministers, senators, or representatives. It's the power takers and the powerful who are favored and honored and followed. Yet even these are called to praise God! There is a limit to their power and status.

In this sense they are democratized in that their summons is no different from the summons of the rank and file. They too are called to praise God, which is to submit to God (cf. Rev. 21:24). All of humanity—high and low, well-born and barely born, those who are old with their best days behind them and those who are young with promise stretched out before them—all, not just some, are called to render praise to God. For after all, our existence by him and our dependence upon him is no different from the inanimate objects of space spinning in the far unreached and unseen corners of his vast cosmos.

So then, all creation—animate and inanimate—sings the being of God, rings with praises to God, shouts out in its various ways that God is God and all things belong to him—no matter how whole, or how broken and torn apart, or how seemingly disconnected from him they appear to be.

Yes, everything in creation belongs to Yahweh and exists to praise him! In the context of discussing the cosmic reality of praise, Karl Barth states: "The praise of the man who knows God might seem small and insignificant amid this mighty chorus. But the writers of the Old and New Testaments certainly did not look at it like that."[4] The pinnacle of praise, in fact, is the redeemed of the Lord, which brings us now to the last two verses.

II.   THE REDEEMED AND THEIR PRAISE (PS. 148:13–14)

Verse 13 is like a bridge between the general humanity of verses 11–12 and the redeemed who are singled out in the last two verses. It reads:

Let them praise the name of the Lord, for His name alone is exalted;
His glory is above the earth and heaven.

---

[4]   Karl Barth, *Church Dogmatics,* III.4, Ed. G. W. Bromiley and T. F. Torrance, trans. A. T. Mackay, T. H. L. Parker, H. Knight, H. A. Kennedy, J. Marks (Peabody, MA: Hendrickson Publishers, 2010), 74.

The redeemed who deliberately and knowingly render praise to God on account of what he's done for them both by creating them *and* by re-creating (i.e., delivering, saving, renewing) them.

Verse 13 is an Old Testament equivalent to the opening of the Lord's prayer: "Our Father who art in heaven, hallowed be Thy name" (Matt. 6:9). Notice how closely it matches our verse: "Let them praise the name of the Lord, for His name alone is exalted; His glory is above earth and heaven."

In other words, why do the redeemed praise God? Because his name (character springing from his being) is exalted! His glory is above earth and heaven, meaning God is above all, sovereignly reigning over all and worthy of praise from the pinnacle of his creation. This means praise from his new-creation people—the redeemed. Yes, the redeemed praise him because they know exactly what it is that the Lord has done for his people.

Verse 14 continues this theme:

And He has lifted up a horn for His people, praise for all His god-ly ones; even for the sons of Israel, a people near to Him. Praise the Lord!

When the Bible speaks about God lifting up a horn for his people, it's typically the image of victory in warfare. It's a picture of God going to battle, of God going forward in all his unmatched strength like a ram using its horn to conquer its enemies. This is God going to battle for us so that we can belong to him, so that we can be near him!

The movement of the psalm shows that the ultimate expression of God's sovereign majesty is *not* in the creation of the world (vv. 1–12) but is in the creation of *his* people from within this world who are uniquely set apart to worship him. The redemption of his people is *praise for all his saints.* Unending praise!

Verse 14 alludes to Deuteronomy 10:21–22, where Moses reminds Israel of the promises made to Abraham and the consequences of those very promises in their lives as those delivered by the mighty hand of God from Egypt. Moses says to Israel about the God of their forefathers:

He is your praise [!] and He is your God; who has done these great and awesome things for you which your eyes have seen. Your fathers went down to Egypt seventy persons in all, and now the Lord your God has made you as numerous as the stars of heaven.

Against the odds, God redeemed his people Israel. He took a good-as-dead clan and gave them life, with hope and a future. He delivered them from death, from evil, from tyranny, from their enemy, which is why Moses says, "He is your praise and He is your God."

In verse 14 our psalmist draws on this experience. God's horn (salvation) *is* the praise of his people! His redeemed people, who, by the way, are more numerous than the stars of the heavens, which already praise God by virtue of their existence and dependence on God—how much more so the redeemed!

The Lord's redeemed are (re-)created by the power of God's delivering horn to be a people near to him. This means a people who draw near to him in worship, wholeheartedly praising him and doing so verbally!

The Lord draws near to us to save us so that we can draw near to be with him to praise and worship him. Once again, the ultimate expression of God's sovereign majesty is *not* the creation of the world. Rather, it is the creation of his people from this riven world who worship him—give him praise—forever and ever.

That's why, of all the gatherings you can go to and participate in, of all the arenas of life where people shout out their praises in support of their favorite teams, or bands, or causes, or celebrities, the praise of God is greatest. Although these other events might be necessary, fun, and horizontally valued, they do not remotely reach the level of what is going on every Lord's Day as the people of God congregate communally as the capstone of God's creation to give expression of their praise to the one and only God!

My church meets at the Heritage Hall in Massachusetts, and it is aptly named, since its heritage is not a mere three hundred years old, but goes all the way back to the psalmist and to Moses and to Abraham and to the promises the eternal God made to him, which are *Yes* and *Amen* in Jesus who delivered us from our sin so we can praise God forever.

We are new stars of the sky.
Near to God.
Forever heeding the call to praise God.
Praise the Lord!

Conclusions

1. God has delivered us from death, evil, tyranny, and our enemies, which is why he is our praise and he is our God.
2. The Lord draws near to us to save us so that we can draw near to be with him—to praise and worship him.
3. Worshiping God is the most important thing we can do—praise the Lord!

Study Questions and Discussion Starters

1. This psalm divides itself into two parts. What is the psalmist trying to teach us in each of these two parts, and how are the two related to each other? What is the function of the ninefold repetition of the word "all" in this psalm?
2. What spectacular photo of the earth and our moon did the spacecraft orbiting the ringed planet Saturn send back to us from more than 900 million miles away? What emotions did that picture evoke in you? How does that compare to what the psalmist felt in this psalm?
3. What does the image of God "lifting up a horn" for his people mean? How do we apply that image to our own day? What historical allusion does verse 14 make to what Moses wrote earlier?
4. How is praise for the creation of our universe and our being related to praise to God for our redemption in this psalm? How can we show the same praise for this double aspect of God's gift to us?
5. Discuss how important to each of us is the fact that our heritage goes back to Abraham, Isaac, Jacob, and David as well as to Calvary and Easter Sunday morning?

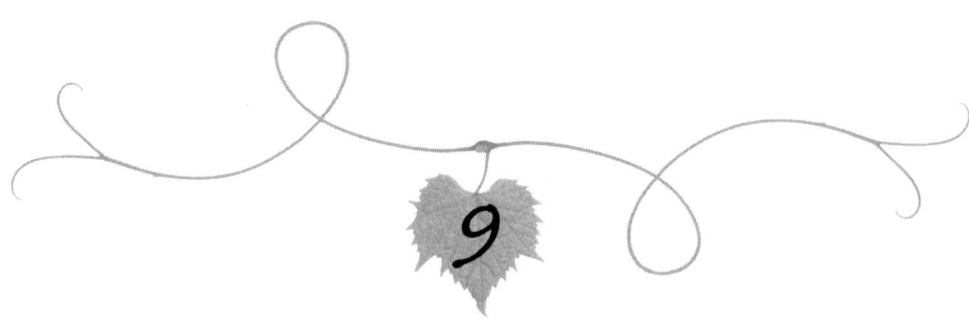

Getting the Facts Straight about God and Creation

Job 38–39

Walter C. Kaiser Jr.

W e're told they lead an uncomplicated life, grazing on grass, leaves, and cactus, basking in the sun, and napping nearly sixteen hours per day. A slow metabolism and large internal stores of water mean they can survive up to a year without eating or drinking. These giant tortoises are the longest-lived of all vertebrates, averaging more than one hundred years. The oldest on record lived to be 152. They are also the world's largest tortoises, with some specimens exceeding five feet (1.5 meters) in length and reaching 550 pounds (250 kilograms). Of course, the Galápagos tortoises are but one among many rare and remote species discovered in the days following Darwin's arrival in the Galápagos Islands in 1835.[1] A wild and crazy menagerie, it seemed, awaited discovery by Darwin.

Oft times, however, all too many just do not know what they are talking about when they try to speak on the topic of the origins of the universe. In an attempt to assume a more scientific stance, some put on airs, just as Job attempted to do (cf. Job 38:2). But Yahweh had to confront Job out of the depths of the storm that accompanied his own presence and words with the same question that must be posed to those who presume they know how the universe was formed in all its intricacies: "Who darkens my design [of creation/purpose] with a cloud of thoughtless words?" (as Moffatt paraphrased verse 2).

---

[1] "Galápagos Tortoise," National Geographic, accessed December 10, 2013, http://animals.nationalgeographic.com/animals/reptiles/galapagos-tortoise/.

In this case, apparently it was the biblical character of Job who was talking way beyond his capabilities, or to put it more bluntly, who was speaking out of his own ignorance. Therefore, Yahweh had to call him up short to allow time for some sense and balance to enter his thinking. Sometimes, this same kind of calling our own thinking short is necessary if we are to make room for the presence of the word of God in our thinking.

Yahweh's challenge to Job, in the face of such insolence on Job's part, was: "Gird up your loins. . . . I will ask you, and you tell me" (v. 3, my translation). The expression to "gird up one's loins" was a figurative way of saying, "Prepare yourself for the strenuous and difficult questioning I am going to put you through." This expression may have come from girding on one's sword to get ready for battle, but C. H. Gordon found it instead to be an allusion to the ancient sport of belt-wrestling, where one contestant would attempt to unfasten the belted sword of another contestant. But the point is clear: If Job was demanding an opportunity to argue his case before God, then he had better thoroughly prepare himself, because God himself would be his inquisitor. This was not to be an easy or short contest to say the least!

As William Henry Green described chapters 38–42 of Job, these chapters are "beyond all comparison the most sublime portion of this wonderful book."[2] Green went on to say, "[God] has no intention of placing himself at the bar of His creatures, and erecting them into judges of His conduct."[3]

Job had more to learn than the answer as to why all this suffering was happening to him at this time. Elihu, the fourth of Job's so-called comforters, prepared Job for the coming of the Lord, who followed Elihu and confronted him with a battery of questions that drew a total blank from Job on all his attempted answers. Thus, we come to the high point in the book of Job and its quest to find some type of explanation for the problem of suffering and evil, especially as Job was experiencing it.

---

[2] William Henry Green, *The Argument of the Book of Job Unfolded* (1874 reprint; Minneapolis: James & Klock, 1977), 285.

[3] Ibid., 286.

Focal Point:	38:4
	"Where were you when I laid the earth's foundations? Tell me, if you understand."
Homiletical Keyword:	Answers
Interrogative:	What? (What answers can we give to any mortal's involvement in creating the world?)

INTRODUCTION (JOB 38:1–3)

I. WERE ANY MORTALS PRESENT WHEN GOD LAID THE FOUNDATIONS OF THE WORLD? (JOB 38:4–7)

II. WERE ANY MORTALS HELPING GOD GATHER THE SEA TOGETHER? (JOB 38:8–11)

III. WERE ANY MORTALS INVOLVED IN CREATING LIGHT FOR THE EARTH? (JOB 38:12–15, 19–21)

IV. HAVE ANY MORTALS JOURNEYED TO THE UNDERWORLD? (JOB 38:16–18)

V. DO ANY MORTALS UNDERSTAND THE POWER AND MYSTERY OF THE STORM, THE STARS, OR THE CLOUDS? (JOB 38:22–38)

VI. HAVE ANY MORTALS ASSISTED GOD IN THE CREATION OF ANIMALS? (JOB 38:39–39:30)

INTRODUCTION (JOB 38:1–3)

The speeches of Elihu, the youngest of the four "comforters," hinted at the fact that Yahweh would address Job himself. Thus, we come to what some regard as the most sublime poetry in this whole book. Even though the previous discourses in this book have been marked by searching and earnest thoughts, often posed with beauty and force, nevertheless, the Lord's words to Job have a mark of grandeur and majesty about them that has not been seen heretofore, for it is such speech as is worthy of deity alone.

Job had feared that if he appeared in court before God, his terror would so intimidate him that he would not be able to represent the issues he posed in his question adequately before the God of the universe (9:34; 13:21). However, Job's constant passion was to somehow have a face-to-face meeting with God and to ask him why he was suffering so much (13:15, 20, 24). If Job could not do this, his final challenge was this: could God present his case for singling him out and put it into writing or even present it in person to Job (31:35–37)? But for Job to expect God to appear in person was indeed both a mark of presumptuousness and real chutzpah on his part. Even Elihu had warned him against this expectation: "It is not [proper] for a mortal to set a time to come before El in litigation" (34:23, my translation). But Job persisted in his request!

As the discourse between Job and the Lord begins, it might seem as if the words of the Lord have no particular relevance to Job and his situation. Therefore, the question would seem to be, what does the magnificence of God have to do with the dilemma that Job in his suffering was facing? But was that not the whole point? God's discourse was not offered as an answer to the mystery of Job's suffering, or as a justification for the divine providence shown toward mortals in general. God will not allow himself to be put in the dock at the pleasure of his creatures merely to justify his actions toward them. Mortals have no right to censure God or his ways. God moves on an altogether different plane, for he is a sovereign Lord who is accountable to no other being but to himself.

Instead, Job has been subjected to the unremitting assaults of Satan, yet he has successfully withstood them as God had predicted. Even though the accuser of the brethren, that is, Satan himself, has done everything in his power to make Job forsake the Lord and his worship, Job has remained conspicuously firm in his stance of serving God as he declared, "I know that my redeemer lives" (Job 19:25). Thus, none of Satan's assaults had worked to detract him from his fear of God.

Verse 1 of chapter 38 begins as if Elihu had not spoken, for no rejoinders or comments are given to Elihu or his speeches, in distinction from the responses to the three earlier "comforters." God began by announcing his name as Yahweh, not his generic name of "El" or "Eloah," used by the other speakers. Moreover, Yahweh spoke "out of the storm," which might bring to Job's mind the "mighty wind" (1:19), which presumably was responsible for taking the lives of his ten children. Accordingly, storms may destroy, but they may also be the means by which the word of God is heard by mortals (Ps. 29:3–9).

As the lightning, the thunder, and the tempest veiled the majesty of Yahweh, who was steadily approaching Job, there came a voice from the center of the storm: "Who is this that darkens design [Hebrew *'esah*] with a cloud of thoughtless words?" (38:2, Moffatt's translation). The word "darkens" had been used in 37:19 to indicate ignorance, but Yahweh was not after information or knowledge; instead, he wanted to know who had dared to obscure his wise plan or purpose by words that were devoid of understanding or respect for God himself. What were his abilities? What was his claim to give a censure to the divine proceedings? Did this bold person have any idea where history was going and what the plan for the future was? That person had better get ready to pick up his robe and prepare for action in a debate by tucking that long robe under the belt around his waist, for Yahweh had some tough questions for such a pre-sumptuous man to answer.

I.   Were Any Mortals Present When God Laid the Foundations of the World? (Job 38:4–7)

This was only the first of a series of questions that Yahweh had for so bold an accuser of his work in providence as Job. There is more than irony in the voice of Yahweh as he went on to ask: "Tell me if you have understanding on these things!" (v. 4b). Who was it who laid the foundations for the earth? Who stretched a measuring line over it? What were these foundations fastened to? Or, who laid the cornerstone for the earth when all the morning stars sang together and all the angels shouted for joy (vv. 6–7)?

Job had not even been born as yet, nor had any other mortal either, for the Lord acted totally alone as the triune God. And the "morning stars" were part of the heavenly hosts or armies that Yahweh of Hosts is sovereign over. True, there are figurative and poetic parts to the questions Yahweh was asking, but it was also a reality that just as surely depicted God as the master builder, even when he used appropriate analogies, such as the footers or cornerstone on which to establish the whole earth.

II.   Were Any Mortals Helping God Gather the Sea Together? (Job 38:8–11)

Yahweh moves the questions from who was there to help him with the anchors of the earth to who helped him with the seas. In verses 8–11, there is a call to deal with the oceans and the seas with all their power and force. Who was it that built hedges and put boundaries on the sea, as if the sea were stopped behind doors (v. 8a)? Genesis 1:9 records how the waters were gathered together into one place as the dry land appeared, but neither Job, nor any other mortal was present to help or direct the action for that event either. Yahweh, as a matter of fact, will muzzle Job, with his bravado talk, just as he muzzled the sea and set proper boundaries for both the sea and now for Job. All must bow before the power of God manifested in bringing the sea into being and under God's control.

The sea is described as if it were a newborn child who was conceived behind doors (v. 8b) and wrapped around with a garment of clouds and thick darkness as its swaddling baby clothes. But it was at that time that Yahweh also set the limits to which the sea could ever transgress on the dry land (v. 10) with its proud waves. God, through the prophet Jeremiah, taught the same concept:

> I made the sand a boundary for the sea, an everlasting boundary it cannot cross. The waves may roll, but they cannot prevail; they may roar, but they cannot cross it. (Jer. 5:22)

Although storms may, from time to time, encroach temporarily on the integrity of the shoreline, the beach eventually wins and remains the line between the land and the sea. That is by order and decree from the creative hand of God.

III.   Were Any Mortals Involved in Creating Light for the Earth? (Job 38:12–15, 19–21)

On the fourth workday of creation, God made the two great lights: the greater light to rule the day and the lesser light to rule the night (Gen. 1:16). Notice that there is a purposeful avoidance of the Hebrew and Semitic names for the sun and the moon (Hebrew *shemesh,* "sun," and *yeraach,* "moon"), so as not to be guilty of setting forth the sun and the moon as idols and objects for worship, which is how the pagan neighbors of Israel regarded these bodies and their similar names. So Yahweh pressed Job further: "Have you ever told the dawn to get to its post?" (v. 12, my translation). Mortals cannot command the sun to rise or, for that matter, the darkness of night to come. Even the wicked scatter as the dawn rises, and they run for cover in a hiding place like cockroaches race for cover when the lights are suddenly snapped on.

The upraised hand (v. 15) is much like the clenched fist in a cocked arm and is called in Hebrew "the high hand," which represents arrogance and defiance against Yahweh. All these signs of rebellion, however, are undone when the dawn appears. A new day is once more inaugurated by God.

In verses 19–21, Yahweh asks Job where light and darkness live? Here the light and the darkness are personified to make the question even more vivid. In fact, light and darkness were separated on the first day of creation (Gen. 1:6). But since Job, it appears, is not going to be able to answer the question, the pressure increases as he is bombarded with a series of five more questions. Tell Yahweh which way to go to find the abode of light; tell him where darkness resides. Does Job know the way to either of these places? Then verse 21, with a note of sarcasm adds, "Since you are one of the oldest men of the community [we guess Job may have been about seventy or more at this time], you must have been there at creation" (my translation). However, what is the lifetime of Job in comparison to the eons that had perhaps preceded him during God's work in creation, or even in the entirety of the eternality of God? Job is reduced to silence and awe before the Awesome One of all creation.

IV.   HAVE ANY MORTALS JOURNEYED TO THE UNDERWORLD? (JOB 38:16–18)

To add to the fund of Job's lack of knowledge, Yahweh asks five more questions of him. Has he been to the "springs of the sea"? (v. 16a). Has he gone to "the recesses of the deep"? (v. 16b). Has anyone shown him the "gates of death" (or the "gates of the shadow of death") (v. 17)? Has he surveyed the "vast expanses of the earth" (v. 18a)? All these areas are off-limits for mortals, including Job. So what was all the fuss this mortal named Job was making? Even if he had traveled several hundred miles, he certainly knew very little about the vastness of what God had made.

V.   Do Any Mortals Understand the Power and Mystery of the Storm, the Stars, or the Clouds? (Job 38:22–38)

In verses 22–30 Yahweh gives one of his longest speeches that focuses on the storm with all of its power, mystery, and unpredictability. Elihu (37:1–13) and Job (6:16; 28:26) have each previously pointed to the effects of the storm, as seen in its effects of lightning, thunder, snow, and ice. But now it is God's turn to ask the questions.

Each element of the weather has been assigned a special role in the providence of God. The word rendered "storehouses" (or "treasuries") is rendered "arsenal" in Jeremiah 50:25. Thus, the rain, the snow, and the hail were kept in store, as if in warehouse arsenals, to be used by God as his weapons when needed. For example, did he not use hail in the seventh plague that fell on Pharaoh and Egypt (Exod. 9:22–26), and did he not rain hail on the fleeing Amorites in Joshua's conquest of the land of Canaan so that more died of the hailstones than from the onslaught of Joshua and his troops (Josh. 10:11)? Will the Lord not use hail again in the last days as hundred-pound hailstones fall on humanity as the plague of the seventh angel in Revelation 16:21 is unloosed?

Job apparently has no answer to any of these questions either. Just as he had no answer for the weather-related inquires about the snow and the hail, so he offers none in response to interrogations about the place from which lightning is dispersed and the east wind is scattered over the earth. Nor does he offer any explanation for the way that the torrents of rain cut gorges into the landscape or the way it plotted the routes taken by thunderstorms in the skies (v. 25).

Some may wish to question why the rain falls on a desert, where no one lives and where few are able to profit from its watering of the dry land (v. 26), but that again is only from an immediately observational point of view. Who knows where some of that rain will end up—perhaps in an oasis or in a spring somewhere. That is a matter for God to know even if we mortals are ignorant of its paths.

In verses 28–29 a new metaphor is used, for here God is depicted as the father and mother who provide the moisture, even by sending the dew during the dry season. Even the ice and the frost are from God, yet it occasionally comes in that mysterious form that is as hard as stone (vv. 29b–30), that is, it comes as frozen ice. God's design in all of these weather-related forms of his creation is to manipulate the weather for either his gracious or destructive end, but it is his to use and to work! Could Job recall how he had assisted in any of this? Of course not!

Likewise, the constellations and the stars (vv. 31–33) are governed by celestial laws that no mortal originally authorized nor now maintains. It was on the fourth workday of creation (Gen. 1:16) that God created the stars; thus, Pleiades and Orion, two of the best known of the constellations, are examples of what God has done. But the point is the same once again: Job had nothing to do with the administration or the formation of the earth in the previous verses; likewise, he had nothing to do with the formation or regulation of the skies or the stars. They too are solely under divine jurisdiction.

The questioning of Job continues under this welter of interrogation. By now it has been established that Job was not responsible for any of the clouds, the rain, or the lightning (vv. 34–38). But just to make sure, Job is asked pointedly: Did he ever raise his voice and thereby call down rain on the land (v. 34)? Did he ever summon the bolts of lightning and they in turn report back to Job saying, "Here we are" (v. 35)? Surely Job does not possess that kind of wisdom, understanding, or power to "tip over the water jars of the heavens" (v. 37)—a wonderful figure of speech for the fact that all rain is stored up by God for release at his command. Job was left speechless and dried up!

VI.   HAVE ANY MORTALS ASSISTED GOD IN THE CREATION OF ANIMALS? (JOB 38:39–39:30)

"Beginning with verse 39," Robert Alden comments, "God took Job on a guided tour of his menagerie, pointing out to him those species that were especially wild, rare, or remote. The questions continue, not to demean Job, but to glorify God."[4]

Lions, the kings of the jungle, did their own hunting for food, for Yahweh had taught them how to "lie in wait in the thicket" (v. 40). It was not Job who had taught them! In the same way, God provided the raven with food as its young cried out to God, not to Job (v. 41). Notice that the young ravens "wander about for lack of food" (v. 41c), for since their parents do not supply them with food, they would die apart from God's guidance of their behavioral traits to provide for themselves!

[4] Robert L. Alden, *Job*, New American Commentary (Nashville: Broadman & Holman, 1993), 381.

Does the man from Uz know anything about the life-giving power of birth in the mountain goats that roamed in small herds around En Gedi ("Spring of the Goats")? These elusive animals of the rocky terrain usually do not give away the place of their birth, the duration of their gestation period, or even the place where they deliver their young. But it seems no sooner had they crouched down and brought forth their young that the labor pains were all over, and the next thing it seemed was that the offspring were thriving and growing strong as off they went to be on their own without returning (39:3–4). It was God who established the life cycle of these animals and who had sustained them, not Job or anyone else.

If Job still wanted to keep his interview with God, then Yahweh had more questions for him. In verses 5–8 of chapter 39, Yahweh wants Job to tell him who untied the wild donkey's ropes and let him go free (v. 5). This question is a little on the ridiculous side, but it is one intended in part to humble Job. The answer of course is God did this. God also gave the wasteland (v. 6, Hebrew 'arabah) as the wild donkey's home. This Hebrew word is still used for the depression that reaches from the south end of the Dead Sea all the way to the Gulf of Aqaba, known as the Arabah.

In order to demonstrate the humor in all this, the Lord asks Job another question: "Can you place this wild donkey in any urban setting, with all of its noise and commotion, and hear owners of their domestic counterparts shout orders to them?" (v. 7, my translation). Yahweh is the one who frees creatures such as these and gives them a place to range and to forage in search of any green thing as the price of its freedom (v. 8).

Yahweh has seven more questions for Job in verses 9–12 as he raises the habits of the wild oxen, which has a will that cannot be tamed or trusted by humans. This large bovine animal, with huge pointed horns, was not built to give up its freedom by submitting to a harness suited to plow or to disc up the land (v. 10). But for all of the animal's fabled strength, it could just as well turn ferociously on the one trying to tame it and seriously hurt the farmer or even kill him.

Yahweh moves on to depict the silliest of all animals, in verses 13–18: the ostrich. This time there are no questions for Job, perhaps as a moment of comic relief; therefore, God refers to one of his creations as something he made for his joy and our entertainment. This huge, lanky bird is known for its speed as well as its apparent stupidity; it cares for the thick-shelled eggs it deposits in the sand, yet it leaves them often with almost absent-minded abandonment (v. 15). The stork, in contrast, is a kindly and loving bird—the exact opposite of the ostrich (v. 16), which originally flourished on the steppes of northern Arabia. What the ostrich lacks is God-given wisdom (v. 17), but there is one gift that this bird does possess: when she spreads her stubby feathers to run (v. 18), she can reach speeds of forty miles per hour, often outdistancing even a horse.

Since the passage raises the subject of horses in the end of the last pericope, Yahweh asks Job about horses in verses 19–25. What about the horse is it that Job has personally contributed to its creation? Is it the horse's strength? Or is it his flowing mane? Perhaps it is his ability to leap? What is it, Job? In fact, none of these qualities, much less the horse itself, could be attributed to Job. That animal was afraid of nothing (v. 22), especially the sword of battle. Let that animal hear the blast of the trumpet and capture the scent of battle, and that horse was more than ready for the fray of the battle (v. 25).

Finally, Yahweh pointed to the hawk and the eagle, for what the lion was as the king of the beasts, so these two birds were the kings of the avian realm. The Hebrew word for "hawk" could also be rendered "falcon" or "harrier." And even though the word "eagle" represents several species in the Bible, this bird is legendary for its strength, its speed, and its ability to spot prey at great distances and promptly take it as it wings its way in its grandeur of flight and dives toward its objective. The question to Job is, were you responsible for any of the amazing feats of these birds?

Yahweh's first interrogation of Job finally ends in 39:30, and the questions ranged from the creation of the cosmos to the providential care for the king of beasts and the king of the birds. Job is no longer so sure as he once was about having his much-sought-after interview with God. In light of Yahweh's questions, he must feel downright stupid. Perhaps it is time for him to be silent and ponder how much there is about which he had no idea how it worked or came into being. His case is dwarfed into insignificance in the face of the magnificence of the Creator and all he has made. God is magnificently great!

CONCLUSIONS

1. Yahweh's wisdom always has exceeded that of any mortal. God had to show to Job things he never even dreamed of.

2. There is a pattern to what God shows Job, which from the outside would seem like a wild order of nature and its creatures. But Yahweh takes Job round and round in the display of his handiwork in order to get him to be silent long enough to realize that what he does not know should humble him to be more ready to trust the Lord who made everything and who continues to providentially care for it all.

3. For the first time, Job realizes that he has gone too far in his protest. It was altogether too brash of him to find fault with Yahweh. He never should have insisted on his own understanding. He never should have accused Yahweh of injustice.

4. There is only one thing left for Job to do: confess that "I am unworthy. . . . I have no answer. . . . I will say no more" (40:4–5). God has spoken and there is nothing more to say—by anyone!

STUDY QUESTIONS AND DISCUSSION STARTERS

1. What were some of the questions (along with the verses) that Yahweh addressed to Job about his work in creating the world? What did God mean when he asked Job to "gird up [his] loins" if he was going to begin to answer the Lord?

2. What did Yahweh's discourse on creation have to do with Job's problem as to why he was suffering? What was God's point, then, if it did not address the problem of Job's immediate suffering?

3. Who were the morning stars that sang together as the foundations of the earth were set up by the Lord (38: 4–7)?

4. What four questions did God bombard Job with about light and darkness (38:19–20)? What was the Lord trying to get Job to see?

5. What two constellations are mentioned in 38:31–33, and what point does God make with Job about their formation?

6. How does God reduce to silence the man from Uz when he inquires if Job assisted him in the creation of the animals (38:39–39:30)?

7. Discuss how wide-ranging Yahweh's questions of Job were and what that tells us about God's role in creation.

10

JESUS AND THE NEW GENESIS ADVENT

MATTHEW 1:1–17

Dorington G. Little

An increasingly popular personal pursuit, especially in light of the expansion of the Internet, is genealogy. It is interesting to study one's family tree, tracking down the ancestors, tracing the family roots. And it's not just the names but also the details about these long-forgotten relatives, such as their lives, loves, leanings, pursuits, and problems.

My aunt is the genealogist in our family. In her research she discovered that my grandfather really wasn't who we thought he was; the name on his birth certificate is not the name he went by as an adult. Why, when, and how this changed nobody knows, though, as you can imagine, there is no shortage of speculation. The result is that he's a man of some mystery.

For many, genealogical pursuits remain rather boring, unless, of course, they concern one's own family. Given that, what's the worst text a pastor can preach on—*all* four Sundays of Advent, no less? Why, surely it is the genealogy of Jesus, which is set before us in all its droning detail in Matthew 1:1–17. How homiletically wretched is it, we're told, to open the glorious story of the Lord Jesus with a lengthy, dull, and dreary list of dauntingly unpronounceable names?[1] What could possibly be of interest? Does it concern us, much less matter to us, that Jesus' lineage as outlined by Matthew traces back to promises given to an ancient man thousands of years before Jesus arrived on the scene? Do promises made to a man residing in one of the most cosmopolitan parts of the ancient Near East,

---

[1] The SLJ Institute, S. Lewis Johnson, "The Genealogy of Christ," accessed November 29, 2012, http://www.sljinstitute.net/sermons/new%20testament/gospels/matthew/matthew_master.html#birth_and_childhood_of_jesus.

who is asked to pack up and leave the equivalent of New York City and move to a place comparable to Last Chance, New Mexico, even remotely interest us?

Can it be of any relevance to us at all that the rise and fall, the ascent and descent of Israel, its astounding upward climb from nothingness to regional domination followed by its nasty spiral down, down, down into crushing defeat and despairing exile in Babylon—that all this is compacted into the forty-two generations highlighted in these verses?

Can it even remotely pique our curiosity to consider that the names in Matthew 1 include wealthy kings in palatial splendor, whose assets far exceeded in terms of personal holdings, land, buying power, and raw power even that of the wealthiest of our generation? And yet, with no apology whatsoever, the list marches on with names of homeless and utterly destitute sojourners—people who can't rub two shekels together, listed shoulder to shoulder with forgotten kings in Jesus' genealogy.

How strange it is to discover, wading through this list, that it brings us face to face with the record of the godly and the despicable, the strong and the frail, the faithful and the faithless, the snake and the dove, the famous and the infamous, the popular and the obscure, powerful generals and the generally powerless. Truly, this gallery of Jews and Gentiles, with both men and women, is often far earthier than it is overtly heavenly. And as for the surprising inclusion of certain women, it lists the outcast, despised, violated, seriously underprivileged, and pitiable before abruptly and amazingly ending with a virgin, *by whom was born Jesus, who is called Christ.*

All this prepares us to see how God, out of faithfulness to his incredible promises, intentionally works through not just the best but also through the worst of people, times, and circumstances. This is because our God is not deterred by anyone or anything in bringing to fruition his gracious eternal purposes for humanity, all of which point to and culminate in the birth of a virtually indigent and destitute baby whose name is Jesus.

Focal Point: v. 1
                                     "The book of the genealogy
                                     of Jesus the Messiah, the
                                     son of David, the son of
                                     Abraham."

Homiletical Keywords:	Genealogy of Jesus Christ
Interrogative:	Who? (Who is Jesus?)

I.   JESUS IS FULLY HUMAN (MATT. 1:1)

II.   JESUS IS THE CLIMAX OF ISRAEL'S HISTORY (MATT. 1:17)

III. JESUS BOTH SIGNALS AND BRINGS ABOUT THE NEW BEGINNING

I.   JESUS IS FULLY HUMAN (MATT. 1:1)

The opening verse of the Gospel is meant to bring important introductory ideas to our attention, facts about Jesus that perhaps we never realized or have simply forgotten. It reads:

> The book of the genealogy of Jesus the Messiah, the son of David, the son of Abraham.

This verse answers the question, who is Jesus? From the outset Matthew desires us to grasp that *Jesus is fully human.* The forty-two generations listed here are important for many reasons, including the fact that these are names of real people who lived in time and space. They are participants in and contributors to a specific people's history in world history. Although many of their names mean little or nothing to us by virtue of the thousands of years that separate us from them (as well as on account of our biblical illiteracy), nevertheless, because Jesus was born into a family with deep roots in the mists of time, we are thereby assured by virtue of this genealogy that though fully divine, *Jesus is also fully human as we are!* He is not an approximation *to* it, nor even a facsimile *of* it, but a full participant *in* it. Jesus became a full member of our humanity with all of its nitty-gritty, inglorious as well as glorious nature, and yet he is without sin.

> Since then the children share in flesh and blood, He Himself likewise also partook of the same, that through death He might render powerless him who had the power of death, that is, the devil. (Heb. 2:14)

What did Jesus share? Jesus took on our flesh and blood, our humanity. Why did he share it? He did so, so that by his death he might destroy "him who holds the power of death"—the devil—and free those who all their lives were held in slavery by their fear of death. Who, therefore, does Jesus help? Angels? No! Abraham's descendants? Yes! Jesus came to help real people—people like us with all their sins and fears and gnawing despairs and nagging concerns and ever-present ponderings and irreconcilable differences, those who are stalked by death with its multiple calling cards. We are the ones Jesus came to help, whose humanity he came to share. For this reason he had to be made like his brothers in every way, in order that he might become a merciful and faithful high priest in service to God, that he might make atonement for the sins of the people (Heb. 2:17).

The Bible makes it clear that Jesus had to become one of us in order to atone for us. Jesus became fully human, yet without sin, in order to accomplish God's redemptive purpose. Thus one of the primary goals of Matthew's genealogy is to show us that this is so. This is the book of the genealogy of *Jesus* Christ. Jesus is his historical everyday human name, and *Christ* (Anointed One) is his title. Jesus, or *Yeshua* (Hebrew), is the equivalent of the Old Testament name "Joshua," which means "Yahweh is salvation." Jesus brings us precisely that. Jesus is aptly named because he "will save His people from their sins" (Matt. 1:21).

II. JESUS IS THE CLIMAX OF ISRAEL'S HISTORY (MATT. 1:17)

This brings us to the next point Matthew wants us to ponder through his genealogy. Jesus is fully human and, as such, *Jesus is the climax of Israel's history*. Let's accelerate to the very end of the genealogy and look at verse 17:

> Therefore all the generations from Abraham to David are fourteen generations; and from David to the deportation to Babylon fourteen generations; and from the deportation to Babylon to the time of Christ fourteen generations.

Verse 1 asserts and verse 17 confirms that the gospel, and in fact all of Israel's history, is ultimately about Jesus "who is called Christ" (v. 16). While there is much more to say about this, I want to draw your attention to it now because the conclusion of the genealogy sums up what is being taught throughout the entire genealogy. Namely, we're taken through this list of names from Abraham—whom God called and set apart as father of the Hebrews, and to whom was promised descendants as numerous as the stars in the night sky and the granules of sand on the ocean shore—all the way to King David whose throne God swore would never be vacant. Then from David, with all of his successes and painful failures, we continue the march of ancient names through the precipitous descent into exile in Babylon followed by return to the Promised Land until Jesus Christ comes onto the human scene.

Jesus saves his people from their sins, because although they've been back in their physical land for centuries, nevertheless, they remain in exile spiritually. Jesus is the Christ, the Anointed One of God, the Messiah. His title declares that he is the true and eternal king, not just of God's people but of all history, since his people will include Gentiles as well as Jews in accordance with the promises made to Abraham. In this way everything in the genealogy leads to Christ and everyone in the genealogy points to Christ.

Now, in this connection, before we move to the last point we should ask, why does Matthew like the number "fourteen"?

> Therefore all the generations from Abraham to David are *fourteen* generations; and from David to the deportation to Babylon *fourteen* generations; and from the deportation to Babylon to the time of Christ *fourteen* generations. (v. 17, emphasis mine)

The number fourteen is more than a convenient structural device Matthew uses to chart out family lineage, and it is more than a way to mark out the sections of Israel's history. Specifically, the number symbolically communicates the idea of fulfillment or consummation.[2] Bear in mind, the Hebrews did not count using Arabic numbers as we do. That is, they didn't have a separate set of characters for numbers. Instead, the twenty-three consonants of their alphabet did double duty, serving both as letters and as numbers.[3] Numerically speaking, then, David's name in Hebrew is *D* [*dalet*]–*W* [*waw*]–*D* [*dalet*]. By this, "Da'wid" is the combination

---

[2] Joel Kennedy, *The Recapitulation of Israel* (Tübingen: Mohr Siebeck, 2008), 74n213.

[3] Gary D. Pratico and Miles V. Van Pelt, *Basics of Biblical Hebrew* (Grand Rapids: Zondervan, 2001), 111–16.

of the fourth letter of the alphabet (and thus the numeral equivalent of 4) plus the sixth letter (6) plus the fourth (4). Consequently, Matthew's readers knew as they looked at King David's name that it added up to 14.

Additionally, because Jesus, who is called Christ, comes at the end of no less than three sets of 14, we are thereby meant to see that Christ is the culminating Davidic king of Israel's history. Even more than that, as Matthew's Gospel will teach, Jesus Christ is the king of all of history. Jesus is the exclamation point on God's faithfulness to his promises and to his people, which is why Christ stands dramatically and climactically at the end of Matthew's genealogy! The order of Israel's history, with all of its high and low points, its ascent, descent into exile, re-ascent from exile, and subsequent languishing in expectation of Messianic deliverance through the providence of God, leads us to this point, to this person, and to this purpose. Christ is the exalted sum of it all! Fully human? Yes! King over all? Absolutely! Jesus is the King whose mission is to Israel and a world that is painfully lost, but by God's grace and plan is not abandoned!

III. Jesus Both Signals and Brings About the New Beginning

All of what has been said so far is in service of one last key point. Jesus is fully human, and Jesus is the climax of Israel's history, for *Jesus both signals and brings about the new beginning.*

Please return to verse 1, which states: "The book of the genealogy of Jesus Christ." Literally it reads "book of beginning of Jesus Christ," or "book of genesis of Jesus Christ." With this Matthew deliberately uses the words that are used for the title of the first book of the Bible and then again in Genesis 2:4 and Genesis 5:1. In the latter, Moses writes, "This is the book of the generations of Adam. In the day when God created man, He made him in the likeness of God." From the intentional echo and anticipation in Matthew's word choice, we are meant to see that what God formerly did to bring about the creation of humanity, he later does through Jesus to bring about the *new creation!* Just as Genesis tells the story of one beginning, so now the Gospel of Matthew tells the story of another beginning. The Gospel narrates the record of the new beginning to overturn the old order. It is the account of the new beginning launched by the coming of this unexpected baby to impoverished parents. It is about the baby who would grow to be a man, die on a cross, and then, most astoundingly, rise from the dead. Jesus ushers in the new beginning that overturns the effects of the fall, reverses its curse, and redeems the fallen to forge a new humanity. It is the story of a new people, from among all the peoples of the earth in accordance with the promises made long ago to father Abraham, who himself was the recipient of a miracle baby.

By beginning his Gospel in this way Matthew is proclaiming that a new beginning has arrived in the incarnation of a newborn under the banner of the world's true king. After his resurrection, Jesus, with kingly authority, will tell his newly formed people:

> All authority has been given to Me in heaven and on earth. Go there-
> fore and make disciples of all the nations baptizing them in the name
> of the Father and the Son and the Holy Spirit teaching them to ob-
> serve all that I commanded you; and lo, I am with you always, even
> to the end of the age. (Matt. 28:19–20)

Little wonder that all the Gospels, not just Matthew's, subtly or not so subtly, put a new creation emphasis right at or near the start of their writing.[4] John's Gospel is of course the most obvious in this regard with his echoes of the Genesis creation narrative leading to new creation realities:

> In the beginning was the Word, and the Word was with God, and
> the Word was God. He was in the beginning with God. (John 1:1–2)

Again, why do the writers emphasize this? It is because Jesus came to our broken planet to commence the new creation! In the process there is no glossing over the not-so-admirable, often dysfunctional and disordered members in his own particular family ancestry. This underscores for us that the unsavory people in Jesus' lineage are the very sorts of people he came to save. These names—of idolatrous, self-serving, greedy, and immoral people—are not simply historical time markers in flesh and blood but are emblematic of all humanity's deepest need. They evidence our plight, thus our need for divine intervention to be born again as a new creation, for there is no self-salvation.

By the way, did you notice what's missing in verse 16? The expected but missing line is "and Joseph, the husband of Mary, begat Jesus." Instead, we read Mary's name followed by the feminine case for the relative

---

[4] Matthew 1:1; cf. also Mark 1:1, Luke 3:23–38 (tracing from Jesus to Adam), and John 1:1–18.

pronoun, "by whom." This highlights for us that the birth of Jesus has absolutely nothing to do with Joseph, but has everything to do with God and Mary. Jesus is miraculously conceived, as verses 18–25 go on to show! Joseph is excluded from the biological process! The verse then inserts God as the subject of the verb "by whom was born" to make the direct connection from God to Mary and Jesus, not to Joseph and Jesus.[5] Yes, Joseph is the husband of Mary, but he is not the father of Jesus in the physical sense.

Why is this so? It is because Israel's messy history alone cannot produce the Messiah. Intervention is required. Divine intervention! In this way from the very first page of the Gospel the genesis of Jesus is presented as connected with a people, who, nevertheless, could not produce him. He came into this race, was of it, born of a virgin, yet was sinlessly distinct from it. He is fully human and fully divine. It takes the miraculous to come and save us and to internally re-create us. It takes nothing less than the sinless Lamb of God to bear our sin and ultimately remake us to be what God intends us to become. Apart from Jesus Christ there is no new genesis.

Indeed, we are meant to consider that, like Mary, we too are weighed down by the scandal of our sin. We too are outsiders to God and alienated from each other. We need intervention from above by the one who comes here below. Matthew's genealogy underscores that the arrival of the infant Jesus is not about a sentimental, syrupy, "Ah, will you look at that, the virgin Mary had a baby!" Instead, it is about Jesus Christ whose extraordinary coming is into the matrix of our perplexing human existence. Jesus is the one whose ancestors summarize our current plight, whose arrival signals our new beginning, whose temporarily tragic story reverses the seemingly irreversible trajectory of our own, and whose intervention saves us from our sin. Jesus does all this so we can become the King of King's new-creation kin. Amen!

Conclusions

1.   In general, genealogical passages stir little interest in our hearts and minds. But quite the opposite is meant to be the case when we open the Gospel of Matthew. There, captured in an intentional

---

[5] The verb is a divine passive.

list of names presented in intentional form, Matthew's genealogy introduces us to God's new creation work of taking our fallen, broken humanity and redeeming us into a people of his own possession. Far from being boring, Matthew's opening is powerful and compelling, depicting the drama of our redemption!

STUDY QUESTIONS AND DISCUSSION STARTERS

1. Name some of the reasons why the list of forty-two generations in the genealogy of Jesus is so important both to Jesus and to us?
2. Why was it necessary for Jesus to share our flesh and blood with us? Why did he share it with us, and for what purpose?
3. Why was Matthew's genealogy arranged in sets of fourteen? From where did Matthew borrow the first words or title for his book? What is the significance of that borrowing and usage? How does that title compare with the way the Gospel of John begins?
4. Why does verse 16 use Mary's name followed by the feminine case for the relative pronoun "whom"? What does this say about Joseph and his role in the birth of Jesus?
5. Discuss the importance and the wonder of Jesus' coming into the world and being born in the womb of a mortal and going through the process of growing up with our flesh and blood.

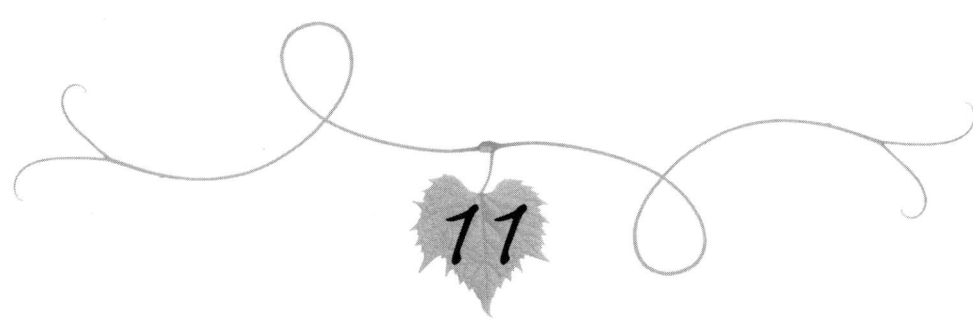

THE NEW HEAVENS AND THE NEW EARTH

ISAIAH 65:17–25 AND 66:22–24

Walter C. Kaiser Jr.

*T*he same Lord who made the original heavens and earth is the Lord who will also make these same heavens and the earth new once more. Therefore, to deny that he is in a real sense the maker of heaven and earth in the first place is to open up one's self for denying that he will also be the maker of the new heavens and the new earth! But just as surely as Scripture teaches that the living God brought the original creation into order by the word of his mouth (Ps. 33:6, 9), so it is assured that our Lord can make anew and renew this same creation by his power in a future day.

The two great passages that introduce the topic of the new heavens and the new earth are Isaiah 65:17–25 and 66:22–24. But this same teaching, as well as the New Testament references in 2 Peter 3:10–13 and Revelation 21, was also taught by a number of pious Jewish teachers and others beginning with the early church leaders.

In anticipation of the kingdom of God, which embraces the new heavens and the new earth, the present heavens and earth will undergo a transformation so that all evil and unrighteousness can be removed prior to the appearance of the new heavens and the new earth. Most conservative Protestant theologians of every shade and variety are persuaded that before that final age begins, there will come of necessity some drastic changes in the present natural order. The most graphic statement of this change is given in 2 Peter 3:10–13:

But the day of the Lord will come like a thief. The heavens will disappear with a roar; the elements will be destroyed by fire, and the earth and everything in it will be laid bare [or burned up]. Since everything will be destroyed in this way, what kind of people ought you to be? You ought to live holy and godly lives as you look forward to the day of God and speed its coming. That day will bring about the destruction of the heavens by fire, and the elements will melt in the heat. But in keeping with his promise we are looking forward to a new heaven and a new earth in which righteousness dwells.

It is important to note that the end of verse 10 is usually rendered by an additional marginal note in some Bibles to read "shall be discovered" or "laid bare" (Greek *eurethesetai*) instead of the reading of "shall be burned up" (Greek *katakaesetai*). The manuscript evidence for this change of being "discovered" (i.e., "being laid bare") is strong; however, it is difficult to say which text captures what it is that Peter meant, for the prophets also mention fire as part of that great work of God in the day of the Lord. In keeping with this marginal reading in other manuscripts, however, the NIV renders this phrase "will be laid bare," which seems to be the correct text here.

TIMING OF THE CONFLAGRATION

Usually interpreters wrestle with two main problems in 2 Peter 3:10–13 and other texts related to this same topic. First, when will this event take place—at the beginning of the millennium or at the close of those thousand years of the rule and reign of Messiah? Second, what are the extent and the nature of the changes that are anticipated in this conflagration? Will they involve an annihilation or just a renovation of the existing order of creation? And if it is only a renovation, then how drastic will the changes be?

In this chapter we shall advocate the view that the new heavens and new earth will occur at the beginning of the millennium. We shall also try to show that the types of changes introduced in the new heavens and the new earth will be of a limited renovation, rather than a complete annihilation of all existing order.

The view of the timing is the one advocated by the Lutheran Pietistic scholar George N. H. Peters in his extensive, three-volume work titled

The Theocratic Kingdom, and Robert D. Culver in Appendix 1 of his book *Daniel and the Latter Days.*[1] In this chapter we will essentially follow many of the arguments set forth by these two writers.

Many Old Testament prophets describe a period of a great conflagration similar to Peter, and they locate it just before the beginning of the millennial reign of Christ, which is in a period belonging to the times of the second advent of our Lord Jesus. For example:

> I will show wonders in the heavens and on earth, blood and fire and billows of smoke. The sun will be turned to darkness and the moon to blood before the coming of the great and dreadful day of the Lord. (Joel 2:30–31)

> I will send my messenger, who will prepare the way before me. Then suddenly the Lord you are seeking will come to his temple; the messenger of the covenant, whom you desire, will come, says the Lord Almighty. But who can endure the day of his coming? Who can stand when he appears? For he will be like a refiner's fire or a launderer's soap. He will sit as a refiner and purifier of silver. (Mal. 3:1–3a)

> "Surely the day is coming; it will burn like a furnace. All the arrogant and every evildoer will be stubble, and that day that is coming will set them on fire," says the Lord Almighty. (Mal. 4:1)

Already in the time when the apostle Peter wrote it, it is clear that the subject of the coming day of the Lord with its judgment of purifying fires was not a new or unheard-of subject, for 2 Peter's audience was anticipating or "look[ing] forward to the day of God" (2 Peter 3:12). Therefore, the Jewish audience, who knew their Old Testament, surely anticipated that a fiery judgment from God would precede the appearance of the kingdom of God, as well as its new heavens and new earth.

Not only was that day of the Lord to be preceded by fire, but it also would witness an enormous heavenly shake-up, for "the heavens will disappear with a roar" (2 Peter 3:10). This also was part of the teaching of the Old Testament prophets:

---

[1] George N. H. Peters, *The Theocratic Kingdom,* 3 vols. (Grand Rapids: Kregel, 1952); Robert D. Culver, *Daniel and the Latter Days* (Chicago: Moody, 1979).

All the stars in the sky will be dissolved and the heavens rolled up like a scroll; all the starry host will fall like withered leaves from the vine, like shriveled figs from the fig tree. (Isa. 34:4)

This is what the Lord Almighty says: "In a little while I will once more shake the heavens and the earth, the sea and the dry land. I will shake all nations, and what is desired of all nations will come, and I will fill this house with glory," says the Lord Almighty. (Hag. 2:6–7).

The Lord will roar from Zion and thunder from Jerusalem; the earth and the heavens will tremble. But the Lord will be a refuge for his people, a stronghold for the people of Israel. (Joel 3:16)

See, the day of the Lord is coming. . . . Therefore, I will make the heavens tremble; and the earth will shake from its place at the wrath of the Lord Almighty, in the day of his burning anger. (Isa. 13:9a, 13)

Lift up your eyes to the heavens, look at the earth beneath; the heavens will vanish like smoke, the earth will wear out like a garment and its inhabitants die like flies. But my salvation will last forever, my righteousness will never fail. (Isa. 51:6)

To these verses can be added Hebrews 12:25–27, which, in part, quotes Haggai 2:6:

See to it that you do not refuse him who speaks. If they did not escape when they refused him who warned them on earth, how much less will we, if we turn away from him who warns us from heaven? At that time his voice shook the earth, but now he has promised, "Once more I will shake not only the earth, but also the heavens." The words "once more" indicate the removing of what can be shaken—that is, created things—so that what cannot be shaken may remain.

All these cosmic disturbances seem to occur at the beginning of the millennium and not at the end of those thousand years. The passage just quoted in Hebrews should clarify the timing issue.

The Nature and Extent of the Coming Conflagration

The cosmic disturbances announced in 2 Peter 3:10 consist primarily of the death of all wicked men and women at the time of the second coming of our Lord Jesus Christ. But there will also be changes that occur in the inanimate world, and similar changes will occur in the plant and animal realms.

The word that our Lord Jesus used to describe these changes is "regeneration" (Greek *parlingensia*):

> Jesus said to them, "Truly, I tell you, at the renewal [regeneration] of all things, when the Son of Man sits on his glorious throne, you who have followed me will sit on twelve thrones, judging the twelve tribes of Israel. (Matt. 19:28)

This word *regeneration* also is rendered as "new birth," which is how the apostle Paul used it in Titus 3:5. Paul also described this new life that has come as a result of the new birth in Christ as a "new creation" (2 Cor. 5:17), for all the old things had passed away and all things had become new. Thus, this word signals the restoration of all things back to their primal estate as they had existed prior to the fall of Adam and Eve. It is true, of course, that even after the believer has experienced the new birth, sin still resides in each of us. But sin will be completely removed when we see the Lord face to face (1 Thess. 3:13).

It is important, therefore, to note that the words of 2 Peter 3:10 do not require a total annihilation of the old heavens and the old earth; rather, Peter declared under the inspiration of our Lord that the old heavens and earth "will pass away" (Greek *pareleusontai* from the root *paraerchomai*). This word is never used to mean annihilate; instead, its meaning is to pass from one space or time to another. Even if the concepts of "to be dissolved" (Greek *luthesetai*) or "to be burned up" (Greek *katakaesetai*) are included from the Textus Receptus manuscripts, this still does not amount to an annihilation of the old heavens and the old earth. It could simply be the purification of what already existed.

In fact, there are many passages that speak of the perpetuity of the heavens and the earth. If they were to be annihilated or obliterated, the Scriptures could not have taught their removal, as some have argued, on the basis of these following texts:

[God] set the earth on its foundations; it can never be moved. (Ps. 104:5)

Praise him, sun and moon, praise him, all you shining stars. Praise him, you highest heavens and you waters above the skies. Let them praise the name of the Lord, for at his command they were created, and he established them for ever and ever—he has issued a decree that will never pass away. (Ps. 148:3–6)

This is what the Lord says, he who appoints the sun to shine by day, who decrees the moon and the stars to shine by night, who stirs up the sea so that its waves roar—the Lord Almighty is his name. (Jer. 31:35)

As Culver correctly observed, "To insist that the materials of earth must be cremated [i.e., obliterated] in order to remove sin is to insist on an erroneous doctrine of sin [i.e., as if the seat of sin were in the stuff of] matter, rather than in the spirits of free agents."[2] Culver went on to note that Genesis 8:22 declares categorically that as long as the earth remains, the order of nature will remain constant and without interruption: "As long as the earth endures, seedtime and harvest, cold and heat, summer and winter, day and night will never cease."

Even in those texts that seem to require a complete dissolution of the earth and a change in nature, such as in the time of Noah's flood, not everything was destroyed. Eight humans in that flood were provided a way of escape on the ark, along with the animals that were preserved in the ark. Of course, water life also escaped dissolution.

Likewise, the coming conflagration and regeneration at the second coming of Christ will involve the death of all living wicked men, as the apostle Paul announced:

For the secret power of lawlessness is already at work; but the one who now holds it back will continue to do so till he is taken out of the way. And then the lawless one will be revealed, whom the Lord Jesus will overthrow with the breath of his mouth and destroy by the splendor of his coming. The coming of the lawless one will be in accordance with how Satan works. He will use all sorts of displays of power through signs and wonders that serve the lie, and all the ways

---

[2] Culver, *Daniel,* 184–85.

that wickedness deceives those who are perishing. They perish because they refused to love the truth and so be saved. (2 Thess. 2:7–10)

Peter, in agreement with Isaiah 34:4, taught that the heavens would pass away with a roar (i.e., great noise) and that the elements would be dissolved in an enormous heat. The word "elements" (Greek *stoicheia*) may refer to heavenly bodies, but this word is also used five times outside of 2 Peter to refer to the false moral or spiritual "rudiments" found in false religions or false philosophies of this world order. However, if the word has reference to actual elements in the material world, then it refers to the wide changes anticipated in the physical world that would precede the establishment of the Lord's kingdom.

The New Heavens and the New Earth

The coming kingdom of God that will emerge as a result of this conflagration and cosmic upsets will feature a renewal of the heavens and the earth that results in what is now called a new heaven and a new earth. The two most important texts that support this conclusion are Isaiah 65:17–25 and 66:22–24. These texts read:

> "See, I will create a new heavens and a new earth. The former things will not be remembered, nor will they come to mind. But be glad and rejoice forever in what I will create, for I will create Jerusalem to be a delight and its people a joy. I will rejoice over Jerusalem and take delight in my people; the sound of weeping and of crying will be heard in it no more. Never again will there be in it an infant who lives but a few days, or an old man who does not live out his years; the one who dies at a hundred will be thought a mere child; the one who fails to reach a hundred will be considered accursed. They will build houses and dwell in them; they will plant vineyards and eat their fruit. No longer will they build houses and others live in them, or plant and others eat. For as the days of a tree, so will be the days of my people; my chosen ones will long enjoy the works of their hands. They will not toil in vain, nor will they bear children doomed to misfortune; for they will be a people blessed by the Lord, they and their descendants with them. Before they call I will answer; while they are still speaking I will hear. The wolf and the lamb will feed together, and the lion will eat straw like an ox, and dust will

be the serpent's food. They will neither harm nor destroy on all my holy mountain," says the Lord. (Isa. 65:17–25)

"As the new heavens and the new earth that I make will endure before me," declares the Lord, "so will your name and your descendants endure. From one New Moon to another and from one Sabbath to another, all mankind will come and bow down before me," says the Lord. "And they will go out and look upon the dead bodies of those who rebelled against me; their worm will not die, nor will their fire be quenched, and they will be loathsome to all mankind." (Isa. 66:22–24)

So what are we to understand by this title of a "new heavens and a new earth?" We have seen thus far that the material aspect of the earth will experience a transformation, or conflagration, that will remove evil and all that is wrong and opposed to the rule and reign of God that will be the rule for the millennium. After that, as Revelation 11:15 summed it up: "The kingdom of this world will become the kingdom of our Lord and his Messiah," for our Lord's kingdom will supersede all earthly kingdoms of all earthly potentates of all times.

The word "new" (Hebrew *hadashim* or *hadashah*), however, does not necessarily mean something entirely new, but denotes a renewal, or restoration, of that which already existed. This meaning can be illustrated when the same word is used in Hebrew for the new moon, a new heart, or the new creature in Christ. It is, of course, the same moon, the same heart, and the same person, but ones that are renewed. This seems to illustrate what is meant in this situation of a new heavens and a new earth!

Accordingly, what is claimed here in the teaching of the new heavens and the new earth is the physical restoration of the cosmos and the restoration of the Davidic-Messianic kingdom, which will supersede all the earthly empires of mortals as described in Daniel 2 and 7. Some point to Revelation 21:1, where it says, "and there was no more sea," as an indication that the meaning to be attached to these new heavens and new earth is symbolic and spiritual, which some interpreters see as the extension of the gospel that finds this symbol to be completed in fulfillment only in the third heaven. But the texts in Isaiah 65:17, 18, and 66:22, along with 2 Peter 3:10, firmly locate the fulfillment in the future with a fully physical relationship to this earth. It is better to take the primary and leading idea of these texts than it is to follow a figurative, or symbolic, sense with a meaning that moves away from the intent of the writer of this Scripture. Thus, when the renewal of the created order is realized once again, it will be a glorious transformation of the natural world in a real and historical manner, not just a spiritual or symbolic restoration.

It must be noticed that 2 Peter 3:13 and Revelation 21:1 clearly depend on the two passages in Isaiah, for they relate that all that happens here will be in the future and it will be "in keeping with his [God's] promise." Since there is no other possible text of such a promise to which Peter could be alluding, then he too was locating these new heavens and new earth as an event that succeeds the conflagration and regeneration.

Focal Point:	Isaiah 65:17 "See, I will create new heavens and a new earth. The former things will not be remembered, nor will they come to mind."
Homiletical Keyword:	Changes
Interrogative:	What? (What are the changes that God will make when he creates the new heavens and the new earth?)

I.   THE TRANSCENDENT CREATORSHIP OF GOD WILL CHANGE THE UNIVERSE (ISA. 65:17)

II. THE SORROW AND SHAME SIN HAS BROUGHT INTO THE WORLD WILL CHANGE (ISA. 65:18–19)

III. THE LIFE SPAN OF ONLY A FEW DAYS OR YEARS WILL CHANGE (ISA. 65:20)

IV. THE PREVIOUS EVIL OF ROBBING MORTALS OF SEEING THE RESULTS OF THE WORK OF THEIR HANDS WILL CHANGE (ISA. 65:21–24)

V.   THE POISONOUS, DEVOURING, RAVING ASPECTS OF THE FALLEN WORLD WILL BE CHANGED (ISA. 65:25)

VI. . The Old Heavens and Earth Will Change into the Eternal New Heavens and Earth (Isa. 66:22–24)

I. The Transcendent Creatorship of God Will Change the Universe (Isa. 65:17)

"Behold" (or "Look here," "See") introduces a note of surprise that promises that God will intervene and demonstrate his creative power once again. Such a grand picture picks up aspects that have already been given in different parts in Isaiah 11:6–9, 25:6, and 26:15. While it is impossible to say exactly all that will be involved in this new creation, one thing is very clear: God will exercise his power to renew the universe and to banish sin and sorrow forever from here on out.

The same Lord who created the original universe certainly has the ability to remake and renew a new heaven and a new earth. Therefore, the Creator who spoke the original cosmos into being by the word of his mouth (Ps. 33:6, 9) also has the power to bring a renewed heaven and earth where sin with all of its evil work no longer has any dominion over God's people (Rom. 6:14). Thus, "the world to come" (Heb. 2:5) will manifest itself also in the lives of believers, who also will each be a "new creation" (2 Cor. 5:17), renewed by the Holy Spirit of God.

But this will also be a millennial kingdom in which the world will be redeemed and renewed (Rev. 20:4–6), because the first heaven and first earth will have "passed away" (2 Peter 3:13; Rev. 21:1). In so doing, the former world will be forgotten and all the things associated with it will likewise be forgotten.

II. The Sorrow and Shame Sin Has Brought into the World Will Change (Isa. 65:18–19)

God commands his people to rejoice and to be glad because of what he will do when he creates the new heavens and the new earth, as well as what will happen when he creates a new Jerusalem. Three times in verses 18–19 God calls for rejoicing, for his new creation will blot out all our bad memories of the former world and days. He will make all things new!

The apostle John also talked about this new Jerusalem in Revelation 21:1, for he saw it as coming down out of heaven. Some want to debate whether this is merely a transformed Jerusalem or a totally new one. It is not possible to say from these texts, but it will be enough to say it is new and that it is the special work of God.

The Lord himself will rejoice over Jerusalem (v. 19a), which is a marvel in itself, since that city has all too often been the source of grief and disgust to him because of its sin, instead of a source of joy. But that will all be a matter of the past, for now "weeping and crying will be heard in it [Jerusalem] no more" (v. 19d; cf. Isa. 25:8; 35:10; Rev. 21:4). God will wipe away all those tears.

III. THE LIFE SPAN OF ONLY A FEW DAYS OR YEARS WILL CHANGE (ISA. 65:20)

Another reason there will be no more crying or mourning in the kingdom of God is that untimely death will be no more. Therefore, a nursing infant will not live for a mere few days, nor will an old man not live out all his years. If one were to die at a hundred years old, it would be as if he died as a lad or was under a curse (v. 20d). Surely what is taught here is one of conscious exaggeration or hyperbole to make the key point that in God's kingdom there will be no need to weep over the unexpected death of a loved one or to deal with the problem of death. One hundred years would be a short life indeed; so rejoice, for God has a new set of plans for humanity's longevity.

IV. THE PREVIOUS EVIL OF ROBBING MORTALS OF SEEING THE RESULTS OF THE WORK OF THEIR HANDS WILL CHANGE (ISA. 65:21–24)

In the previous creation, as a result of the curses for disobeying the law of God, very often some mortals would not get to enjoy the fruits of their labor. For example, often a man would build a house only to have someone else come along to live in it (v. 21a). Or another man would plant a vineyard and then someone else would eat the fruit of it (v. 21b). It seemed as if mortals were all too often being cut down by death just as they reached what they had thought was only the middle of their lives.

However, in place of all the tears of frustration and futility, God will replace them with songs of praise and thanksgiving to his name. God's men and women will have such stable lives in the kingdom of God that they will be likened to long-lived trees (v. 22c). The blessing of God will rest on God's people and their descendants (v. 23b–c). The frustration and exhausting toil of life in those days of the old creation will be gone (v. 23a) as God's kingdom will be enjoyed to the full.

Moreover, there will be perfect communication with God (v. 24), for so attuned will we all be with the heart of God that even before we call upon the Lord, he will answer. This means he will not only hear, but simultaneously he will take the appropriate action while we are still praying and calling on his name.

V.   THE POISONOUS, DEVOURING, RAVING ASPECTS OF THE FALLEN WORLD WILL BE CHANGED (ISA. 65:25)

This verse appears to be a condensation of Isaiah 11:6–9, with many of the same words being used. Thus, another reason for rejoicing in the new creation God will make is to be seen in the pacification of the harmful aspects of the older creation, which were affected by the fall. The examples used here are those of the wolf and the lamb feeding together with the "lion . . . eat[ing] straw like an ox" (65:25a). This surely signals a whole new world!

Also, the snake that had been condemned to crawl on its belly in the dust for his part in tempting Eve in the fall, is also changed by God. The serpent would "bite the dust" (our idiom) as victory would come from the woman's seed, whose heel, that is, the heel of her seed, would indeed be bitten, but this child of Eve's in turn would trample and crush the head of the serpent, that old dragon, the devil, in total conquest. Therefore, no one, not even the formerly vicious and harmful animals, would hurt or destroy in all God's holy mountain.

VI.   THE OLD HEAVENS AND EARTH WILL CHANGE INTO THE *ETERNAL* NEW HEAVENS AND EARTH (ISA. 66:22–24)

Sin will never again stain the renewed creation as it had the old heavens and earth. God had promised Abraham a name, a seed, children, and a land. But now there is more: all redeemed humanity will go together to Jerusalem periodically to worship the Lord. Moreover, they will see the carnage of the bodies that have rebelled against the Lord and note that their worm does not die nor will the fire on their bodies be subject to being quenched. The sight of their end will be loathsome indeed. But the work of God's new creation will be everlasting and it will endure.

The fact that Scripture attributes the original creation and the renewed creation to the powerful word of the same Lord God, makes it easy to see clearly how believers can summarily reject all theories that attribute the original creation to the processes of natural selection or to something, or someone, other than God. The fact that God is the Creator of both the original and the renewed creation of the new heavens and the new earth shows us that God is the source for both creations. In fact, many of the same terms are used for both creations, so getting one straight should help us to better understand the other as well.

No wonder Scripture teaches us to rejoice in the Lord who has made all things after the counsel of his own will. And he has done all of this by the power of the word of his mouth.

CONCLUSIONS

1. God by himself will create the new heavens and the new earth as he comes to rule and reign in the millennium.
2. No longer will evil, disgrace, and shame hold its guilty hand over our heads, for all believers will be blessed forevermore.
3. The Davidic-Messianic kingdom of our Lord will be preceded by a conflagration, or at least a grand regeneration of all of nature and all sin and evil.
4. Nature itself will be healed as the lion, the lamb, and the serpent lie down and feed together on vegetation without hurting or destroying anything in all God's holy mountain.
5. No longer will men and women toil to build houses or plant vineyards and then die without enjoying the fruits of their labor, for death is now a defeated enemy that our Lord has once and for all removed from his people.

STUDY QUESTIONS AND DISCUSSION STARTERS

1. What is so important for understanding how the promise of a new heavens and a new earth will be brought into existence if we either deny or seriously qualify the fact that the Lord directly created the original universe by the word of his mouth?

2. When will the new heavens and the new earth appear in the future according to the comments made in this book about the Scriptures that teach this doctrine? How do the purifying fires figure into this new heaven and new earth? Which translation is better: "laid bare" or "shall be burned up"?

3. What other events or happenings, besides these fires, will be part of the future day of the Lord according to the Scriptures? Can you name some of these texts?

4. What is improper about the view of sin and evil, according to Culver, that insists that all the elements of the earth must be incinerated, or obliterated, to remove evil?

5. What is probably a more accurate way of rendering the word "new" in "new heavens" and "new earth"? What difference will this translation make?

6. Name some of the changes that will occur in the new heavens and new earth according to Isaiah 65:17–25 and 66:22–24 and 2 Peter 3:10–13. How will these changes in the new creation compare with what we now experience in the original creation?

12

OUR NEW CREATION CONFIDENCE

FOR PROCLAMATION AND LIVING

2 CORINTHIANS 4:6 AND 5:17

Dorington G. Little

*I*n 1913 the idea of venturing into the dense jungles of the Amazon River was simply out of the question, writes Candice Millard.[1] With the exception of a few large and widely spaced rivers, each more than eight hundred miles long, there was a huge blank spot on the map of South America the size of Germany. Within this unexplored *terra incognita* lay the vast tangled expanse of the Amazon rain forest.

So remote and unknown was the Amazon that the first substantial effort to penetrate it (to build a two-hundred-mile-long railroad) ended in utter failure. The railroad was designed to carry the highly prized sap of the rubber tree from the depths of the Amazon to the coast, where it could be shipped to overseas markets. That was the plan. Any promise the railroad held, however, was totally eclipsed by the horrors of building it.

Laborers were so depleted by their working environment and its conditions that they were described as bearded like Crusoe, pallid as anemic women, and speckled with insect bites. There were men who worked where the sun never shone, for its light was stopped by the unbroken green that, except where the big rivers flowed, roofed the whole land.[2]

---

[1] Candice Millard, *The River of Doubt: Theodore Roosevelt's Darkest Journey* (New York: Doubleday, 2005), 21–22.

[2] Ibid., 22.

Little wonder that over the course of five years six thousand men died of disease and starvation, working, as it turns out, on a railroad that was abandoned shortly after completion so that, in effect, they lost their lives for nothing.

Some of the apostle Paul's opponents in Corinth certainly thought his sufferings and ministry were all for naught. Indeed, in their view his sufferings were contrary to the gospel and therefore rendered his ministry illegitimate. The gospel should lead us from triumph to triumph, always onward and upward; a super spirituality vindicated by a prosperous vitality in all aspects of life! Yet, by all accounts, Paul was a man going nowhere with nothing of ultimate value to offer.

Why give him a vote of confidence when it is obvious he was a loser? Look how he suffered. Moreover, listen to his message about a crucified Christ. "Where's the victory in that?" his detractors likely muttered in an effort to undermine and marginalize the apostle's influence and mute his message. "How can that possibly engender any confidence for spiritual living?"

In the face of these detractors Paul asserted they have misunderstood what new creation is and looks like in the hurly-burly of daily living. In turn, this means they didn't grasp the nature of true gospel confidence for ministry. Consequently, as biblical scholar Scott Hafemann explains, Paul's burden in 2 Corinthians is "to make it clear that in his sufferings he is the aroma of the crucified Christ (2:14b–16b); that in the jar of clay that was his weakness Paul carried the treasure of God's glory (4:6–7)."[3]

As he does so, Paul reminds us that both his and our confidence for ministry is directly derived from and linked to the power of creation—a new creation, that is.

Focal Point:	2 Cor. 5:17
	"Therefore, if any man is in Christ, he is a new creature; the old things passed away; behold new things have come."

---

[3] Scott J. Hafemann, *2 Corinthians,* The NIV Application Commentary (Grand Rapids: Zondervan, 2000), 19.

Homiletical Keywords: New Creation

Interrogative: What?
                       (What astounding thing has
                       the Lord done in making
                       new creatures?)

I.   Confidence for Ministry Is Directly Derived from and
     Linked to the Power of the New Creation (2 Cor. 4:6)

II. A New Creature in Christ (2 Cor. 5:17)

———

I.   Confidence for Ministry Is Directly Derived from and
     Linked to the Power of the New Creation (2 Cor. 4:6)

2 Corinthians 4:6 reads as follows:

For God, who said, "Light shall shine out of darkness," is the One
who has shone in our hearts to give the light of the knowledge of
the glory of God in the face of Christ.

The reason Paul didn't lose heart despite his suffering, the reason
he preached Christ Jesus as Lord and only commended himself as being
nothing but a slave for Jesus' sake, was that this former hater and persecutor of the church had been transformed by the mercy of the Lord (4:1).
To be sure, the god of this world—Satan, the anti-creator, the malevolent
agent of de-creation, so to speak—had maliciously blinded the minds
of the unbelieving so that they might not see the light of the gospel of
the glory of Christ, who is the image of God (4:4). But—praise God!—
the Creator and Redeemer intervened to overturn the chaos of sin and
unbelief in order to create new people with new life, of which Paul is
exhibit A.

Given new life solely by God's grace and power, Paul didn't preach a
bogus gospel of human self-sufficiency featuring himself as a swashbuck-
ling man of spiritual power. No, shockingly, Paul was intentionally a servant of the Corinthians! Meaning, the true gospel that he preached was

embodied in his Christlike willingness to consider the needs of others as more important than his own "rights."[4]

How can he do this? How can he put up with the indignities and insults of the Corinthians and the unending maligning of his antagonists? How can he endure it seemingly all the time? More to the question, how can he endure horrific near-death experiences (e.g., 1:8–10; 2:14–16; 4:7–11; 6:4–10; 11:23–28) moment-by-moment while bearing his cross like Jesus?

Paul did it "for Jesus' sake" (4:5b). In other words, he served others even to the point of death no matter what it took because this is how the cross functions. Everything, all the time, was on behalf of Jesus to reveal Jesus. In this way Paul's life and ministry embodied the cross of Christ, which, of course, was only possible because he had become a totally different person from whom he once was, which brings us to verse 6.

Just as the Spirit of God moved over the surface of the waters and God spoke the words "Let there be light" (Gen. 1:2b–3) and there was light, created *ex nihilo,* so too in order to bring his new-creation people into existence, God has creatively spoken once again, banishing the darkness and chaos of sin and alienation. How did he do this? Through his Son!

Through Jesus, God has shone the life-giving power and light of new creation into human hearts. Jesus Christ reveals the glory of God to his people. In short, in the first creation, humanity is made in the image of God, though because of the fall of Adam, that image is distorted and marred. But now, by the power of the cross of Christ bringing about the new creation, we are formed into the image of God in Christ.

We are new creatures destined for the fullness of new creation that awaits us (Rev. 21–22). In the between time, spanning the first and second advents of Christ and empowered by the Spirit of Christ, we live in the in-breaking of the age to come, revealing Jesus to the world around us. Yes, this is a radical change that God has brought to us and has wrought in us.

Think of Paul's own experience in this respect. Saul of Tarsus, a Roman citizen; an educated, erudite, persuasive, multilingual, rising luminary in the school of the Pharisees, a man who is a somebody in the world in which he lives. "There goes Paul," we imagine his peers on the streets of

---

[4] Ibid., 178.

Jerusalem or in the temple courts exclaiming. "He's going to be preeminent one day. Just you watch!"

Sure enough, this man of privilege and increasing power found himself one day heartily condoning the murder by mob of a Christian leader named Stephen. Standing by self-righteously, if not smugly, with the robes of bloodthirsty henchmen collecting in a pile around his feet as they circled, then dove like sharks into frenzy, he lauded their attempts. This is shortly followed by Saul's overseeing the ravaging of the fledgling church, mercilessly entering houses of believers and dragging men and women into prison (Acts 8:3).

Not satisfied with efforts close to home, virtually snorting in his anger, breathing out his own murderous threats against the followers of Jesus, whom he deemed a Messianic pretender, Saul went to the high priest for official letters granting him permission to stamp out the church wherever it may be—to arrest and bind its adherents and bring them back to Jerusalem.

All this because "Paul regarded the proclamation of a crucified Messiah to be so utterly despicable and erroneous that he became convinced that the adherents of this new movement must not be tolerated and that active measures be taken to stop their activities."[5]

So it is we find Saul on his way from Jerusalem, drawing near to Damascus. As the ancient city's structures came into view on the horizon, anticipation of looming arrests quickened his heartbeat. It was noontime when, unexpectedly, a light far brighter than the midday sun flashed around him, stunning him. Crashing to the ground Saul unmistakably heard a voice asking, "Saul, Saul, why are you persecuting me?"[6]

Face in the dirt, perplexed, shaking in fear, by way of a quivering response the persecutor of the church asked, "Who are you, Lord?" The answer from on high to the man groveling down low in the dust? "I am Jesus whom you are persecuting" (Acts 9:5).

When Paul eventually arose from the ground he was wide-eyed but blind. Needing to be led, he was taken into Damascus where in time his vision was restored by the believer Ananias, who laid healing hands

---

[5] Eckhard J. Schnabel, *Early Christian Mission, Volume 2: Paul and the Church* (Downers Grove, IL: InterVarsity Press, 2004), 928.

[6] See Acts 9, 22, and 26 for accounts of Paul's conversion. See also 1 Corinthians 15:8–10 and Galatians 1:13–17.

on him. From thenceforth Paul was commissioned by the resurrected Jesus as his chosen instrument to "bear My name before the Gentiles and kings and sons of Israel; for I will show him how much he must suffer for My name's sake" (Acts 9:15–16 NASB).

II.   A NEW CREATURE IN CHRIST (2 COR. 5:17)

Formerly bound in darkness by Satan, Paul now became a new-creation intervention of Jesus', moving from darkness into the light. This was Paul's conversion—his life-changing encounter with the "light of the knowledge of the glory of God in the face of Christ" (2 Cor. 4:6). The Creator spoke and shone forth and an incredibly hardened heart was made new—transformed—the result of which was a totally new life journey. The former persecutor then gladly suffered for Jesus' sake in order to live forth the cross of Christ. Paul's life-altering Damascus road experience was the foundation of his theological heart and his daily existence as an apostle.

"Instead of opposing Christ," writes David Wells, "Paul submitted to him. Instead of being alienated from God, Paul was reconciled to him. Instead of being spiritually dead, Paul was spiritually alive by means of the Spirit. Instead of assaulting Christians, Paul joined them. Before conversion Paul had not looked beyond Israel. After his conversion Paul took the gospel to the Gentiles."[7]

Paul's call is irreversible; his gospel proclamation is forged and the contours of his cross-shaped ministry divinely mandated. All this is because new life had come to him. Encountering God's glory in Christ was utterly transformative, and he truly was a new creature in Christ. As such, let's now fast-forward to the familiar words of 2 Corinthians 5:17:

> Therefore, if any man is in Christ, he is a new creature; the old things passed away; behold new things have come.

After detailing the nature of his apostolic sufferings and the fullness of his gospel hope in the face of death through the balance of chapter 4 and the beginning of chapter 5 of 2 Corinthians, Paul urged the Corinthians to reconcile with God.

---

[7] David F. Wells, *Turning to God: Biblical Conversion in the Modern World* (Grand Rapids: Baker, 1989), 51.

He readily admits in 5:16 that the way he previously assessed people, even Christ, was wrong. He had believed Christ was weak and his cross a scandal. All who followed such a one were similarly to be scorned and spurned.

But in light of encountering the risen Lord Christ, that fleshly, worldly, analysis is a thing of the past. Christ truly is the Lord, the one who died for all so that those who live might no longer live for themselves, but for him who died and rose on their behalf (v. 15).

As a result, glorious facts have to be faced and embraced. A new, fresh age has dawned and broken into the old, leading to the creation of new life. As such, everyone who is in Christ really is a new creature, just as Paul himself was, which means that the old way of living life and thinking about life is archaic and superseded. It has passed out of existence. Behold, look and see; believe and follow; new things have come!

For the Corinthians the clear imperative was that they must now view their behavior toward each other in light of this new all-encompassing cosmic yet personal reality. Furthermore, they needed to see Paul, amid all his sufferings, as the genuine ambassador of the ministry of Christ's reconciliation—begging, entreating, proclaiming for the Corinthians to be reconciled to God.

Yes, the new age with new life has broken into the old. In Christ, spiritual and moral transformation is not just a potentiality but is the new reality. God made Jesus, who knew no sin, to be sin on our behalf, that we might become the righteousness of God in him (5:21). Corinthians, it is time to live in the power of this new-creation light!

This doesn't mean that they (or we!) live with super-spiritual experiences. Again, it means that life has a new orientation, a new-creation orientation. Christians are being transformed into the very likeness of Jesus—to reflect his character, to serve as he served, thus to love as he loved. Practically speaking, each day Christians must die to self and put the needs of others first, for this is the nature of Christ's love (1 Cor. 13).

Jesus is not just the object of our faith; he is the model for our faith. From his own lips we hear:

> Whoever wishes to become great among you shall be your servant; and whoever wishes to be first among you shall be slave of all. For even the Son of Man did not come to be served, but to serve, and to give His life as a ransom for many. (Mark 10:43b–45)

Jesus does not call his disciples to admire him but to follow him. God's new-creation people do not dictate to their Creator but now live out their new-creation, God-glorifying calling. The day about which Isaiah spoke has gloriously dawned. "Do not call to mind the former things, or ponder things of the past. Behold, I will do something new" (Isa. 43:18–19a). This is the situation in which Paul, the Corinthians, and all believers in Christ now live. Christ died to free us from sin and its power and we have therefore died to our old way of life under the power of sin. A new-creation life is now lived out for others![8] We are being conformed to Christ, who is the image of God in which we were created.

Hence, the more Christlike we become, the more we reflect our true new-creation selves. Philip Hughes wonderfully calls this "Christiformity!"[9] Christiformity is the whole sum and purpose of our creation.[10] By the grace of God, the marred and scarred, shattered and broken, are re-created into something wonderfully new. Christ makes all things new!

In short, this brief overview of these two texts in 2 Corinthians 4 and 5 reveals that the new creation is the unshakeable basis of Paul's confidence—for all he was and did, and for all he wanted the Corinthians to be and do. No less is true for us. It is through the preaching of the gospel of Christ crucified that new creation comes about, and it is through a corresponding cruciform life that new-creation life is displayed.

Winston Churchill, the great statesman and defender of the world against totalitarianism in a time of terrible calamity, was not the least bit interested in Christianity. He attended church when necessary for the sake of England's national morale in a time of war, but he himself resolutely did not profess faith in Christ. In fact, he once wrote his mother, "If the human race ever reaches a stage of development—when religion will cease to assist and comfort mankind—Christianity will be put aside as a crutch which is no longer needed, and man will stand erect on the firm legs of reason."[11]

---

[8] Hafemann, *2 Corinthians,* 241.

[9] Philip Edgcumbe Hughes, *The True Image: The Origin and Destiny of Man in Christ* (Grand Rapids: Eerdmans, 1989), 27.

[10] Ibid., 385.

[11] William Manchester and Paul Reid, *The Last Lion: Winston Spencer Churchill, Defender of the Realm, 1940–1965* (New York: Little, Brown and Company, 2012), 21.

Historians William Manchester and Paul Reid comment that "a Bible rests to this day on Churchill's bedside table at Chartwell, a sight that moves many visitors to conclude he sought guidance in Scripture. He did not. When Lord Moran, spying the Bible, asked Churchill if he read it, he replied, 'Yes, I read it; but only out of curiosity.'"[12]

Churchill, with supreme confidence, preached himself and his views as the answer to most problems and the key to a new world order. Nevertheless, no matter how essential and amazing he was, even such a great man must face the Lord—the Lord, who does not permit self-salvation and boasting except in the cross of Christ alone, the Lord, Jesus Christ, whose gospel is not mere curiosity but is everything. Indeed, it is our only ground of confidence.

CONCLUSIONS

1. As Christians we rejoice in the astounding fact that we are new creations in Christ Jesus.
2. God, in keeping with his promises, has taken away our spiritual blindness and made us alive in Christ with the promise of full and complete transformation on that coming day when we will see him face to face in all his glory and unmatched splendor.

STUDY QUESTIONS AND DISCUSSION STARTERS

1. How does the apostle Paul remind us in 2 Corinthians 4:6 that both his and our confidence for serving our Lord is directly derived from and linked to the power of the new creation?
2. Paul does not present himself as a man who always wins and is the self-sufficient source of his own spiritual power. What does he say and do that is different? How is this related to the new creation in Christ?
3. What change overtook Paul as he was transformed from his old way of acting as a Pharisee prior to his conversion to his new role as a servant of Christ in new churches being planted all over the Mediterranean world?
4. What suffering did Paul face and bear for the sake of Jesus' name?

---

[12] Ibid., 20.

5. According to 2 Corinthians 5:17, in what ways did the life of being a new creature break into the old life of Paul?

6. How does Philip Hughes define "Christiformity"? How did the life of Winston Churchill give the opposite point of view to Christiformity?

EPILOGUE

A CALL AND A CHALLENGE

The revelatory plan of God embraced an "in the beginning," which of course implied an end or a period known as "the last days." Biblical truth is weakened if it focuses solely on the redemptive-historical features of our faith, for then it must avoid or pass over large teaching blocks of Scripture.

The events of these days have conspired to swing the conversation of the believing community back to the question of origins once again. This must not be an insider's conversation that masses its exegetical and research capabilities only on those types of questions that have been on the tops of our agendas up to this point from the mid-twentieth century. These discussions must broaden so that we engage the secular and scientific world at large. They must also be put in the context of what we mean by the new creation each believer is in Christ and what the new heavens and new earth will entail and how they will come about.

But we are especially vulnerable to the huge amount of biblical illiteracy that has overtaken our younger generations. This work is a call for Bible Study groups to set aside a quarter of their annual studies to take on the discussion and review of *Biblical Portraits of Creation*. It is also a challenge to the churches in North America to lead the assault on biblical illiteracy by setting at least one quarter of its yearly preaching ministry aside for considering the doctrine of creation and how it affects our concepts of God's sovereignty, our view of ecology, our praise to God for all he has done in creation, in making us new creatures and how the new order of things will be introduced.

May your journey in this challenge be an enjoyable one that will pay off handsome dividends and be an enjoyable one in the rich study of God's portraits on creation.

Appendix

The Literary Genre of Genesis 1–11

Walter C. Kaiser Jr. [1]

*T*he primary task of the biblical scholar is to unfold the meaning of the text of Scripture as it was originally intended to be understood by the writer of that text. Those ideas, meanings, and truth-intentions, which he had in mind, are the first order of business. Further, if the concept of biblical authority is to be introduced into the discussion, it will only heighten rather than decrease the intensity of the search to go back to that original writer's thought, for he is the man who claims to have heard the revelation of God.

Nowhere is this task filled with more difficulties for the modern biblical scholar than in the first eleven chapters of Genesis. Indeed, the very subjects contained in these chapters and the admittedly long interval of time that separates the writer from the topics he is writing about are enough to keep the researcher busy.

But with the advent of modern destructive higher criticism following Astruc's "clue" in 1753, a new problem was added to the two already mentioned: the alleged variations and repetitions within the narratives themselves. Now, it was not the discipline of higher criticism that was the new feature; rather, the new and objectionable feature was the introduction of a philosophical and historical grid, borrowed from Hegel (the dialectic) and Darwin (evolution applied to religious history), which was laid over the biblical corpus so as to control its "true" sequence, order, and development.

---

[1] This is in the main from an article I wrote in 1969 for the twentieth anniversary of the Evangelical Theological Society. It appeared subsequently in *New Perspectives on the Old Testament,* ed. J. Barton Payne (Waco, TX: Word, 1970), 48–65.

This fallacy has since been corrected and for the most part retracted.[2] Unfortunately, it was the Wellhausen foundation stone and the first floor of a house upon which had been built a second floor of the various source documents distinguished by the criteria of doublets, style, and lexicography. While many contemporary Old Testament scholars agree that the foundation and first story of this house, built by J. Wellhausen, K. H. Graf, and A. Kuenen, has fallen, only a few Jewish and evangelical scholars have investigated the situation to see if the second story with its J, E, D, P, L, K, S source documents has actually remained intact despite the collapse of the foundation. Umberto Cassuto, and now Kenneth A. Kitchen, are two of these who have documented the fact that the source documents did not survive the crash.[3] It is beyond the limits of this appendix to trace this development, but students of the Scriptures are urged to acquaint themselves with the dispassionate presentation of contemporary Near Eastern materials by Kitchen in order to avoid the bottomless pit of subjectivism in this important area of higher criticism.

While source criticism was emerging, another challenge was being prepared as a result of a collection of tablets uncovered in the 1850s by the British Museum. In 1872 George Smith began to publish the contents of a flood story, which he found on one of these tablets that had been excavated from the Ashurbanipal Library in Nineveh. This was followed in 1876 with a publication titled *The Chaldean Account of Creation.*

The next contribution seems to have been a paper that a young American scholar named George A. Barton read in 1890 and later published

---

[2] George E. Wright, ed., *The Bible and the Ancient Near East* (Garden City: Doubleday, 1961). See especially the article by John Bright, "Modern Study of the Old Testament Literature," 13–31. Compare the criticisms of J. Coppens, *The Old Testament and the Critics* (Paterson, NJ: St. Anthony Guild Press, 1952), 52–79; and Moses H. Segal, *The Pentateuch: Its Composition and Its Authorship and Other Biblical Studies* (Jerusalem: Magnes Press, 1967).

[3] Umberto Cassuto, *The Documentary Hypothesis* (Jerusalem: Magnes Press, 1961); and Kenneth A. Kitchen, *Ancient Orient and the Old Testament* (Chicago: Inter-Varsity Press London: Tyndale Press; 1966), 112–38; also Edwin E. Yamauchi, *Composition and Corroboration in Classical and Biblical Studies* (Philadelphia: Presbyterian & Reformed, 1966), 7–38; and J. A. Motyer, *The Revelation of the Divine Name* (London: Tyndale Press, 1955). See also the standard evangelical Old Testament introductions by M. Unger, E. J. Young, G. Archer, and R. K. Harrison.

in 1893, where he connected the Old Testament passages concerning Rahab, Leviathan, Lotan, and the dragon in the Revelation of John with the materials in these Babylonian myths. It would appear that George Barton's work was influential in the thinking of the German scholar Hermann Gunkel, for in 1895 Gunkel continued this line of thought by pointing to a series of poetic texts in the Old Testament, where he found a battle between Yahweh and the various sea monsters named above. This tradition, he affirmed, was the background for the creation story of Genesis, though he argued that it had been purged by a monotheistic faith.

Here we were introduced to our fourth problem: the alleged similarities between the literary form and content of Genesis and the ancient Near Eastern mythologies, particularly the Babylonian mythologies. From these early contributions up to our present day, very few scholars have found it necessary to challenge the validity of these results as a basis for understanding the opening chapters in Genesis.

S. R. Driver, in his commentary on Genesis, did squirm a little, but he settled his fears by saying that any "antecedent difficulty" that he may have felt in tracing the Genesis material on creation to a Babylonian source was "considerably lessened" when he put alongside this the Babylonian similarities to the Genesis flood that seemed to be so obviously borrowed.[4]

These were not the only challenges. Several have been added by our own century: the semantic problem as evidenced in all language that describes the action of God (particularly now in light of the revolt against metaphysical discussions), and the historical problem as seen in the difficulty of historiography to define its task and to validate its material. If these areas are staggering in their implications for current speech and history, surely the task does not become less difficult when it turns to the early chapters of Genesis.

In part, these last two issues in their biblical application await the results of the first four problems posed above. All too often it has been possible to slide back and forth in the argument—for example, to go from the literary form to the documents and from there to some conclusion about the level of truth or type of historiography that one could expect from

---

[4] Samuel R. Driver, *The Book of Genesis,* 11th ed. (London: Methuen & Co., 1920), 80. See also Wilfred G. Lambert, "A New Look at the Babylonian Background of Genesis," *Journal of Theological Studies,* New Series, 16 (1965): 288.

these chapters in Genesis. To be sure, the questions all play their part, but an orderly discussion dictates that we must take one area at a time. Since we believe that the challenge of source criticism is beginning to be met, this chapter proposes to investigate the alleged parallels from the ancient Near Eastern mythologies as to their relevance for the type of literary form and content to be gleaned from the first eleven chapters of Genesis.

One is fully aware that a number of disciplines stand off in the wings awaiting both the opportunity for an exchange of materials and the results of our investigations—not the least are the two mentioned above (semantics and history) and the sciences.

It is with the name and results of Hermann Gunkel that any researcher in Genesis must reckon. As early as 1895 Gunkel began to draw the contrasts between history and the contents of Genesis 1–11.[5] In 1901 he introduced his famous Genesis commentary with these words: "Are the narratives of Genesis history or legend? For the modern historian this is no longer an open question."[6] And so it was. Skinner repeated this controlling thesis in his International Critical Commentary, saying, "We are not entitled to assume a priori: That Israel is an exception to the general rule that a legendary age forms the ideal background of history."[7]

Thus Genesis 1–11, it was assumed, reflected a "pre-literary and uncritical stage of society."[8] The difference between what these chapters reflected and real history, according to Gunkel, could be put into these six points:

1.   Genesis 1–11 originates in oral tradition, while history is found in literate societies and in written documents of actual events.

2.   Genesis 1–11 deals with personal and family stories, while history concerns itself with great events of public interest.

3.   Genesis 1–11 depends on the imagination of the raconteurs, while history must be traced back to firsthand evidence.

---

[5]   Hermann Gunkel, *Schoepfung und Chaos in Urzeit und Endzeit* (1895). A preface to his famous commentary on Genesis is translated into English as *The Legends of Genesis* (New York: Schocken, 1964), 1–12.

[6]   Gunkel, *Legends*, 1

[7]   John Skinner, *A Critical and Exegetical Commentary on Genesis*, 2nd ed. (Edinburgh: T. & T. Clark; Naperville, IL: Allenson, 1963), v.

[8]   Ibid.

4. Genesis 1–11 (and this is the "most significant" criterion) narrates the impossible (i.e., origin of stars after the planets, derivation of all the streams of the earth from a single source, a chronology of 2,666 years from creation to the Exodus, all the animals in the ark, Ararat the highest mountain), whereas history narrates the possible.

5. Genesis 1–11 is poetic by nature and intends to delight, inspire, and elevate, while history is prose that seeks to inform.

6. Genesis 1–11 is different in form from the classical example of true Hebrew historiography in 1 Samuel 9–20 whereas history is identical in form and style to those searching, uncomplimentary documents of David's Court in 1 Samuel 9–20.[9]

Gunkel, of course, did not limit these observations to Genesis 1–11 as we have here, but he certainly meant that they should apply here.

Therefore, under the heavy pressure of the prestigious scholarship of the late nineteenth, twentieth, and the present twentieth-first centuries, the approach has become all but unanimous by now: Genesis 1–11 is primeval history reflecting the Near Eastern origins (mainly Babylonian) from which it was borrowed. Any modern appraisal of this section of Scripture must thereby reflect these philological and mythological connections.

I. THE SUBJECT CONTENT

What are those elements in the Genesis narratives that suggest a connection with the mythology of the ancient Near East and Babylon in particular? Principally, the subjects discussed are common to the literature and culture of both groups. They are as follows:

1. The so-called four accounts of creations (Gen. 1:1–2:4a; Gen. 2:4b–2:25; Prov. 8:22–31; and allusions found in prophetic and poetical books of the Old Testament)

2. The Serpent and the Garden of Eden (Gen. 3; cf. Ezek. 28:12–19)

3. The Cain and Abel conflict (Gen. 4)

4. The Genealogies of Genesis 5 and 11:10–22

---

[9] Hermann Gunkel, *Das Buch Genesis* (1922), viii–xiv; cf. John L. McKenzie, "The Literary Characteristics of Gen. 2–3," *Theological Studies* 15 (1954): 541–72.

5. The sons of god marrying the daughters of men (Gen. 6:1–4)
6. The Flood (Gen. 6:5–9:19)
7. The Curse of Canaan (Gen. 9:20–29)
8. The Table of Nations (Gen. 10)
9. The Tower of Babel (Gen. 11:1–9)

For each of these topics there are parallels to a greater or lesser degree. The two most famous are the *Gilgamesh Epic* (Babylonian flood) and the *Enuma Elish* (Babylonian Genesis). For the garden of Eden there is the Sumerian *Dilmun Poem*, the *Myth of Enki and Ninhursag*, and the Akkadian *Myth of Adapa*. The Cain and Abel story is seen in the contest of *Dumuzi*, the shepherd-god, and *Enkimdu*, the farmer-god. *The Weld-Blundell Prism* or the *Sumerian King List* is said to reflect our genealogical list, while the themes of the sons of god, the ethnological details on Canaan and the seventy nations, and finally the tower of Babel are all seen as being authentically Babylonian or at least Near Eastern in their origin.[10]

The scholarly community is beholden, however, to W. G. Lambert for his masterful article on the Babylonian background to Genesis. Noting how important the *Gilgamesh Epic* is, with its striking examples of parallelism to the Genesis flood story (the episode of the sending out of the birds being one of the most impressive of those parallels), he begins by reevaluating the dates of our alleged prototypes in Sumer and Babylon. Here is the interesting development: The Sumerian prototype dates from 1800 BC, but makes no mention of the birds. Also, the incomplete copy for the earliest known Babylonian text (1600 BC) to date, lacks any reference to the birds. "Thus the only surviving testimony to the most telling parallel," writes Lambert, "happens to be later than the Biblical account, but nevertheless, I hold that there is a certain dependence of the Hebrew writers on a Mesopotamian tradition."[11] Apparently, no copies earlier than 750 BC contain this reference in Tablet XI, which is parallel to Genesis 8:6–12! This might have stirred up S. R. Driver sufficiently to retain his "antecedent difficulty."[12]

---

[10] Theodore H. Caster, "Cosmogony," in *Interpreter's Dictionary of the Bible,* 4 vols., ed. G. A. Buttrick (Nashville: Abingdon, 1962), 1:702.

[11] Lambert, "New Look," 292.

[12] Driver, *The Book of Genesis*, 30. See also Lambert, "New Look," 288.

If this bird episode of the *Gilgamesh Epic* (750 BC) represents the best example of parallelism, there are other examples that rate as a mere superficial comparison. An illustration of this type can be seen in the Cain and Abel comparison with *Enkimdu* and *Dumuzi*. The parallel is said to reflect the ancient feud between the pastoral nomad (here the shepherd-god Dumuzi) and the farmer (farmer-god Enkimdu).

This identification is "extremely flimsy."[13] The Sumerian story has Inanna (same goddess as Ishtar) preferring the hand of the farmer-god, Enkimdu, in marriage, rather than that of Dumuzi. Inanna's brother, the son-god Utu, prefers the latter, but Inanna holds firm and Enkimdu appeases the loser, Dumuzi, with all kinds of gifts.[14]

How can this be the background for the Genesis 4 narrative? As Sarna points out, never does the biblical text disparage the occupation of the farmer, let alone evaluate and compare the two occupations. The contrast is on the quality of the men in their heart attitudes and not on their occupations. Nor is anything said of a marriage, or of appeasing a loser in Genesis. Indeed, the chapter does go on, as Sarna observes, to enumerate just those skills that are generally connected with a pastoral and nomadic culture and places them in the line of Cain, the farmer, namely, cattle-rearing, music, and metallurgy.

II.   The Philological Parallels

Another approach to the relationship of Genesis 1–11 with other Near Eastern accounts involves the philological aspect. Nowhere is this illustrated better than in the much discussed word *tehom* ("the deep") in Genesis 1:2. Typical of the canonical status this discussion has reached is the statement of S. H. Hooke:[15]

[13] Nahum M. Sarna, *Understanding Genesis* (New York: McGraw-Hill, 1966), 28.

[14] Samuel Noah Kramer, *Sumerian Mythology,* rev. ed. (New York: Harper, 1961), 101–3.

[15] Bernard W. Anderson, *Understanding the Old Testament* (New York: Prentice-Hall, 1957), 385n11: "The Hebrew word for 'deep' (*tehom*) is equivalent to the Babylonian word for Tiamat; here we have a distant echo of the mythology of the ancient world." Also, Norman Gottwald, *A Light to the Nations* (New York: Harper, 1959), 457: "The priestly term *tehom*, 'the deep' is linguistically related to the Babylonian Tiamat, goddess of the chaotic deep." And B. Davie Napier,

The Hebrew word used for the chaos of waters, "the deep" is *tehom*, a word which is generally acknowledged to be a Hebrew corruption of the name of the chaos-dragon slain by Marduk before he proceeded to create order out of chaos.[16]

Even though Alexander Heidel dealt with the basic philological facts as long ago as 1942, Old Testament scholarship has been exceedingly slow in facing up to the realities he presented there.[17]

The difficulty of borrowing a feminine Babylonian word and bringing it over into Hebrew unaugmented by any suffformative elements, and locating a guttural letter *h* (*het*) in the middle of the word has never been adequately explained. This observation by Heidel is generally bypassed with some remark about his orthodox motives for observing this feature.[18]

Kitchen also calls the identification and equation of the two terms a "complete fallacy" and points to the fact that *tehom* is common Semitic as shown now by the Ugaritic *thm*, which was known in the early second millennium BC.[19] Moreover, he faults the whole assumption of Hebrew

---

Song of the Vineyard (New York: Harper & Row, 1962), 48–49: "Here [*Enuma Elish*] chaos is represented in the goddess Tiamat, a name perhaps echoed in the Hebrew word for 'deep,' *tehom*."

[16] Sidney H. Hooke, *Middle Eastern Mythology* (Baltimore: Penguin, 1963), 119.

[17] Alexander Heidel, *Babylonian Genesis,* 2nd ed. (Chicago: Phoenix, 1963), 98–101.

[18] Sarna, *Understanding Genesis,* 22, does call to our attention three facts: (a) while *tehom* is not feminine by grammatical form, it does frequently employ a feminine verb or adjective; (b) *tehom* has the characteristics of a proper name since it is used without the definite article; and (c) in Genesis 19:25; Deuteronomy 33:13; and Habakkuk 3:10 we have in poetic address, "*tehom* that crouches below" and "*tehom* crying out." J. Skinner, *A Critical and Exegetical Commentary on Genesis,* 17n214 answered these three arguments by observing that *tehom* is "confined to poetry (except Gen. 1:2; 7:11; 8:2; Deut. 8:7; Amos 7:4). . . . The invariable absence of the article (except with pl. in Ps. 106:9; Isa. 63:13) proves that it is a proper name, but not that it is a personification. The admittedly clear references to personification are in the poetic passages of Gen. 49:25 and Deut. 33:13."

[19] Kitchen, *Ancient Orient and the Old Testament,* 89–90; also see J. V. Kinnier Wilson, in *Documents from Old Testament Times,* ed. D. W. Thomas (New York: Harper, 1961), 14: "The theory that the Hebrew Genesis is genetically related to the Babylonian has long been held . . . and has relied to a large extent on the

dependence on the Babylonian myths on methodological grounds as well. "In the Ancient Near East, the rule is that simple accounts or traditions may give rise (by accretion and embellishment) to elaborate legends, but not vice versa."

Recently Thorkild Jacobsen has made an excellent case for the fact that Marduk means "son of the storm," and therefore his conflict with Tiamat is a battle of the elements: the god of storm, rain, lightning, and thunder versus the goddess of the sea. This same motif occurs at the same time (middle of the second millennium) in the Ugaritic myth of Baal versus Yam. This immediately raises the question of dependence and the direction of the borrowing. Since Canaan supplies the environmental context, because of its proximity to the Mediterranean Sea, whereas Babylon was somewhat removed, Jacobsen concludes that the myth comes from Ugarit and the possibility that the borrowing of the term for "sea" could be just the reverse of that pictured heretofore by Orientalists, that is, Tiamat comes from *tihamatum*.[20]

Now if this identification of *tehom* with Tiamat has fallen on hard times with morphological differences and methodological problems, then the final blow, so it would seem, is again given in Lambert's study. Not only is a watery beginning just one Mesopotamian notion among others, but it is not as commonly attested as is the notion that the earth came first. Neither is it the earliest cosmological idea known to us from the Babylonian sources. The primacy of the earth is known first around 2600 BC; then sometime after 2000 BC the primacy of water is known, followed by the primacy of time about 1700 BC. Lambert concludes that the "watery beginning of Genesis in itself is no evidence of Mesopotamian influence."[21]

Another example of the results yielded by philological studies is found in the word taken to mean "to brood" in Genesis 1:2. This word, Gunkel felt, lent support to a connection with the Phoenician cosmic world-egg

---

much publicized equation of Tiamat with the Hebrew *tehom* 'the deep.' It is now, however, recognized that since the two words have different meanings . . . it is of no importance whether they are etymologically connected or not . . . and that the epic has no connections of any kind at any point with Genesis."

[20] Thorkild Jacobsen, "The Battle Between Marduk and Tiamat," *Journal of the American Oriental Society* 88 (1968): 104–8. See also Laird Harris, "The Bible and Cosmology," *Bulletin of the Evangelical Theological Society* 5 (1962): 14.

[21] Lambert, "New Look," 293.

theory. Now, it turns out that this very word (*rhp*) does occur in Ugaritic and has the same meaning there as it does in Deuteronomy 32:11, where the eagles are said "to hover, flutter or coast" in the air.[22] The imagery here is one of God caring for the forming of the earth just as the young eaglets are dependent on their parents' attention while they soar over them until they are able to fly and fend for themselves.

III. THE MYTHOLOGICAL MOTIF

Recently some have acknowledged the point just made concerning "the deep" and "to flutter" in Genesis 1:2 and have moved on to discuss the conflict of Yahweh versus the chaos monster. Childs puts it this way: "Although the present usage of the word in Genesis 14 has little in common with Tiamat, Gunkel has shown convincingly that the Old Testament does possess traditions in which the *tehom* is connected with a primeval battle which initiates the creation (cf. Isa. 51:9, 10)."[23]

Here again Lambert gathers together the Near Eastern materials and the result is that "the case for a battle as a prelude to God's dividing of the cosmic waters is unproven."[24] While the *Enuma Elish* does have a battle that precedes the division and separation of the waters, the problem is to locate such a battle in Genesis, or even in the poetry of the Old Testament. The reference in Isaiah 51:9–10 clearly alludes to a request that God act in the historic present as he acted in the historic past, when the Red Sea opened up and "the redeemed passed over." The only other convincing example one could suggest is in Psalm 74:13: "Thou didst crush or divide sea by thy strength." Even here, however, there is a lexicographical dispute and Lambert advises us to translate it: "Thou didst set the sea in commotion."[25] The separation does not necessarily imply a conflict in the Near Eastern mythology, for the three Sumerian accounts do it peacefully, as

---

[22] The Ugaritic texts are the *Story of Aqhat or Dan'cl,* Tablet 1:32ff; III: i, 20–21 and 31–32. Note the similarity of subjects for this verb in Deuteronomy 32:11 and Ugaritic: the *nshr* or plural *nshrm,* "eagles."

[23] Brevard S. Childs, *Myth and Reality in the Old Testament,* 2nd ed. (Naperville, IL: Allenson, 1960; London: SCM Press: 1962), 37.

[24] Lambert, "New Look," 294.

[25] Ibid.

do the Hittites, Egyptians, and Phoenicians.[26] Childs had used just such a conflict as his basis for concluding that "the material found in Gen. 1:2 has its roots ultimately in myth."[27]

The search for the mythological background to the Hebrew creation narratives does not seem to be any more successful when it turns to the figure of wisdom in the book of Proverbs, particularly in Proverbs 8:22–31. A recent examination of this theory by R. N. Whybray concludes that mythology is "notably absent" in the wisdom literature of Egypt and Mesopotamia.[28] Indeed, the very name "Wisdom" was never used as a name for any of the gods or goddesses. Although W. F. Albright had suggested a Canaanite goddess of wisdom, principally on the basis of four short passages in the Ugaritic corpus where *hkm* ("wisdom") occurs six times, Whybray complains that everyone is a reference to the wisdom of the high god El. On examination, the alleged mythological features, such as the famous statement that Wisdom built her house on seven pillars (9:1), also fails to yield the expected results. In the example just cited, it turns out that "remains of Phoenician houses from the late third millennium did have roofs supported by seven interior pillars."[29] The detail is not mythological, but rather concrete. Whybray concludes by observing that "the terms used to describe wisdom's origin are metaphorical, not mythological."[30]

The conclusion seems to be building that neither the subject material with its apparent, but unfulfilled, parallelism to ancient Near Eastern mythologies nor the initial lexicographical studies involving words like "the deep" and "to brood" will serve as guides in leading us to the conclusion that the literary genre (*Gattung*) of these chapters is the category of myth.

---

[26] Ibid., 294n2.

[27] Childs, *Myth and Reality,* 37. Also, we acknowledge that in the Canaanite mythology "the battle is not connected with the original creation" and his "Nevertheless," on p. 38n3.

[28] Roger N. Whybray, *Wisdom in Proverbs* (Naperville, IL: Allenson; London: SCM Press, 1965), 82–92, 99–104.

[29] Ibid., 90.

[30] Ibid, 103.

IV. THE SCIENTIFICALLY IMPOSSIBLE

But let us turn to Gunkel's fourth category, the one he finds to be the "most significant." What about those things in Genesis 1–11 that are clearly impossible? To begin with a fairly concrete example, one could point to the obvious reference to iron in Genesis 4:22, well in advance of the Iron Age, which is said to begin not until around 1200 BC.

Without pretending to be able to date this incident to the lives of Cain's descendants, one may remark that the knowledge of working iron is clearly much earlier than 1200 BC. The Hebrew word (*barzel*) appears to be a loan word from the Sumerian *parzillum*.[31] Several finds have added to the importance of this observation. At Tel Asmar,[32] at Dorah in northwest Turkey,[33] and at Catal Hiiyuk,[34] evidence has been uncovered for working in terrestrial iron (as opposed to meteorite iron, which has a different nickel content) as early as 2500 BC for the first two sites and 6500–5800 BC in the last case. Apparently arts and crafts can be mastered and then lost, only to reappear again in another age. One should be hesitant to declare an "impossibility" here.

The genealogies of Genesis 5 and 11 have often been paraded as prime examples of chronological impossibilities. The remedy, however, for this difficulty is to be found in the type of exposure to the biblical genealogies as given, for example, almost a century ago in William Henry Green's epochal article.[35] Green reminds us that these numbers are never totaled and are apparently in a symmetrical form of ten names each, with three sons climaxing each list. He points to the parallel lists in the Bible where obvious omissions can be demonstrated, for example, in 1 Chronicles 6:3–14 and Ezra 7:1–5. Further, when we consider the range of meanings of Old Testament terms such as "generation" (which can

---

[31] See Deimel's *Sumerisches Lexikon,* Heft 2, where he quotes an inscription from Ebeling's *KAR* 1, 185, 3. 1.

[32] Oriental Institute Communications, No. 17, 59–61.

[33] *Illustrated London News* (Nov. 28, 1959), 754.

[34] Kitchen, *Ancient Orient and the Old Testament*, 37n10, where he refers to *Anatolian Studies* 14 (1962–1964), 111–14.

[35] William H. Green, "Primeval Chronology," *Bibliotheca Sacra* (1890), 285–303. Also see Appendix II in John Whitcomb, *Genesis Flood* (Philadelphia: Presbyterian & Reformed, 1966), 474–89.

equal eighty-plus years)[36] "begat," "son of," "father of," she "bore [*yalad*]
a son,"[37] both in the Bible and now in the ancient Near East,[38] we are
delivered from making some foolish occidental mistakes. The most instructive lesson of all can be gleaned from Kohath's descent into Egypt
(Gen. 46:6–11), 480 years (Exod. 12:40) before the Exodus.[39] Now if
Moses was eighty years old at the time of the Exodus (Exod. 7:7), and
no gap is understood (as we believe the evidence above now forces us to
conclude), then the "grandfather" of Moses had in Moses' lifetime 8,600
descendants, 2,750 of which were males between the ages of thirty and
fifty alone (Num. 3:19, 27, 28, 34–36)! Certainly the writers of the Bible
are not that naive!

The only new feature one meets in the Genesis 5 and 11 lists is the
inclusion of the number of years "A" lived before he begat "B" and then
the total number of years A lived. The solution to the question concerning
the function of these numbers was suggested as far back as 1906 by John
H. Raven.[40] Observing, correctly, that Zilpah was credited with "bearing" (*yalad*) her great-grandchildren (Gen. 46:18), while Bilhah "bore"
her grandchildren (46:25), and Canaan "bore" whole nations (10:15–18),
Raven allows that the first number in the formula may mean that "B"
literally was born to "A" or that "B" was a distant descendant born to "A."
If it is the latter case, then "the age of A is his age at the birth of that child
from whom B (eventually) descended."[41]

---

[36] William F. Albright, *The Biblical Period from Abraham to Ezra* (New York:
Harper, 1963), 9n26

[37] Genesis 46:18, 25; Exodus 6:20; Ruth 4:17.

[38] Kitchen, *Ancient Orient and the Old Testament*, 36–41, and the fine docu-
mentation. See also Abraham Malamat, "King Lists of the Old Babylonian Period and Biblical Genealogies," *Journal of the American Oriental Society* 88 (1968):
1163–73. See the remarks of David N. Freedman in *The Bible and the Ancient Near
East*, 206–7.

[39] Green, "Primeval Chronology."

[40] John H. Raven, *Old Testament Introduction* (New York: Revell, 1906),
134–35.

[41] Ibid., 135. Malamat, "King Lists," 170–71, illustrates this telescoping effect
of some twenty generations from Levi to Samuel in the genealogy of Haman in
1 Chronicles 6:33–38 (18–23 Hebrew) down to David's genealogy of the Hammurabi dynasty, U. J. Finkelstein, "The Genealogy of the Hammurabi Dynasty,

Many have seized upon the Genesis 6:1–4 incident, with the sons of god and the daughters of men in cohabitation, as one of the clearest examples of an impossibility in the natural realm leading to the category of myth. We believe this analysis fails to investigate the original meanings signified by the writer's use of the terms "sons of god" and *"nepilim gibborim,"* that is, the so-called giants. The most adequate treatment and solution known to us is the article by Meredith Kline, who calls upon an exegesis of the text in light of the cognate materials from the Near East.[42] To equate sons of god with angels does not tally with the divine response given in verse 3, namely, God's displeasure with the sin of man. The situation is not relieved by seeing in the sons of god a reference to a godly Sethite line as opposed to an ungodly Cainite line in the daughters of men. For while it meets the test of verse 3, it must equivocate on the meaning of men in verses 1 and 2, that is, mankind generically in verse 1 and Cainites specifically in verse 2. Further, why do we find the kind of offspring mentioned in verse 4 if these are just religiously mixed marriages? Kline's solution is to interpret sons of god (*bn il*) in its Eastern setting as a title for nobles, aristocrats, and kings. These sociologically mixed marriages lusted after power and wealth (the *gibborim* as seen in 6:4 equates to Gen. 10:8–10 and 4:19–24), that is, they desired to become "men of a name"—that is, somebodies (cf. Gen. 11:4)! This structure of events, coming as it does before the flood narrative, agrees with the Sumerian Nippur fragment where the flood narrative is also immediately preceded by the lowering of kingship from heaven, and thus it suggests that both could be a historical reflex of the same event in time and space.

Of course, common to all these "impossibilities" is the underlying supposition that the worldview resident in Genesis 1–11 is pre-scientific and primeval. Nowhere can one find a greater unanimity on this point than in those discussions that point, with elaborately labeled diagrams, to a three-storied universe.[43] A flat earth (Isa. 11:12; Rev. 20:8) is capped with a solid firmament or dome (Gen. 1:7, 8, et passim) appropriately

---

Journal of Cuneiform Studies 20 (1966): 95–118, and the upper portion of the Assyrian King list.

[42] Meredith G. Kline, "Divine Kingship and Genesis 6:1–4," *Westminster Theological Journal* 24 (1962): 187–204.

[43] T. H. Caster, "Cosmogony," 1:702. The same illustration is repeated on p. 5 of the same work; also in S. H. Hooke, *In the Beginning*, vol. 4 of the

outfitted with windows (Gen. 7:1, 8:12; 2 Kings 7:2; Isa. 24:18, et passim) and supported by pillars (1 Sam. 2:8; Job 9:6; etc.), stretching upward past sheol and "the deep."

Laird Harris has shown that each step of this diagram depends more on the ingenuity of the modern scholar than it does on the imagination of the original raconteurs.[44] Nowhere does the text state or imply that the *raqia'*, better translated as "expanse," is solid or firm. This latter idea of firmness is derived from the Vulgate *firmamentum* and the Septuagint *stereoma*. S. R. Driver tries to document the dome or canopy effect in his commentary on Genesis 1:6, but he fails to explain the Ezekiel 1 and 10 references, where the word clearly refers to an extended platform on which the throne of Ezekiel's vision rests. As Harris observes, the heavens are also likened to a curtain or a scroll that could be rolled up (Isa. 34:4; 40:22).[45] As for the windows in this vault, which are alleged to let the starlight and rains in, we need only to see what is said to come in through these windows: "barley" in 2 Kings 7:2, "trouble and anguish" in Isaiah 24:18, and "blessings" in Malachi 3:10! Actually, in the 2 Kings passage, God has to make the windows (not just open them) before he can send down the barley! (Note also the distinct Hebrew word used for window, *'arubba,* versus the more common *hallon.*[46])

The subterranean features, including the pillars, sheol, and waters under the earth, on examination also fail to uphold the triple-decked or three-storied universe. The waters under the earth easily qualify as waters below the shoreline where the fish dwell (Deut. 4:18), and *sheol* is a poetic word for "the grave." While some poetic passages describe the foundations of the earth as resting on pillars, we may note that both words are

---

Clarendon Bible (Oxford: Clarendon Press, 1947), 20; Skinner, *A Critical and Exegetical Commentary on Genesis,* 21–22; and Driver, *The Book of Genesis,* 6–7.

[44] R. Laird Harris, "Bible and Cosmology," *Bulletin of the Evangelical Theological Society* 5 (1962): 11–17; "The Meaning of the Word 'Sheol' as Shown by Parallels in Poetic Texts," *Bulletin of the Evangelical Theological Society* 4 (1961): 129–35; "The Mist, the Canopy, and the Rivers of Eden," *Bulletin of the Evangelical Theological Society* 11 (1968): 177–79.

[45] Harris, "Bible and Cosmology," 12; Caster, "Cosmogony," 704, translates *raqi'* as a "strip of metal," mentioning Exodus 39:3, Jeremiah 10:9; but no such meaning can be attested from these ideas of stretching, hammering, or extending.

[46] For supporting evidence, see Harris, "Bible and Cosmology."

used metaphorically (one even continues today); and Job 26:7 even has the earth resting upon nothing!

The primitive view turns out to be an assigned interpretation and not one that was derived from the texts themselves. Nor does it help the case if one alludes to additional examples of alleged naiveté in these chapters—for example, the wet cosmology of Genesis 1:1 versus the dry cosmology of Genesis 2:4b–6;[47] the animal fable of Genesis 3, where the snake talks;[48] the tree of the knowledge of good and evil and the tree of life as containing, so to speak, some sort of mysterious enzymes;[49] and the origin of Eve from the side of man or man from the dust of the earth.[50]

Even the tower of Babel incident is yielding to investigation. Samuel Noah Kramer has recently found a tablet that completes the earlier "Golden Age" passage, and in its completed form it turns out to be a Sumerian story that recalls a time when all men spoke the same tongue.[51]

---

[47] Umberto Cassuto, *A Commentary on the Book of Genesis,* part 1 (Jerusalem: Magnes Press, 1961), 101–4, and by the same author *The Documentary Hypothesis*, 74–78; Derek Kidner, "Genesis 2:5, 6: Wet or Dry?" *Tyndale Bulletin* 17 (1966): 109–14. See note 43 above.

[48] J. Oliver Buswell, *A Systematic Theology of the Christian Religion,* vol. 1 (Grand Rapids: Zondervan, 1962), 264–65, 279–82, where he argues that the grammar supports the rendering, not of a biological reptile (which does not eat dirt and is not the object of the enmity in 3:14), but the serpent—the devil. Creepers are already created in Genesis 1 and declared to be good.

[49] Ibid., 272–79; Geerhardus Vos, *Biblical Theology* (Grand Rapids: Eerdmans, 1954), 37–51; and Arthur H. Lewis "The Localization of the Garden of Eden," *Bulletin of the Evangelical Theological Society* 2 (1968): 169–75.

[50] Caster, "Cosmogony," 705, notes that this connection of woman with the flesh of man cannot be limited to the connection observed by Samuel N. Kramer, *Bulletin of American Schools of Oriental Research* (Supp. Studies No. 1, 1945), 9, in the Enki and Ninhursag epic (TI = "rib" and "life" with NIN.T1 "lady of the rib"). Many other peoples witness the same general connection when the influence of missionaries and the philological similarities "can be reasonably discounted." See also the magnificent demonstration of R. A. Martin, "The Earliest Messianic Interpretation of Gen. 3:15," *Journal of Biblical Literature* 84 (1965): 425–57.

[51] Samuel N. Kramer, "The Babel of Tongues: A Sumerian Version," *Journal of American Oriental Society* 88 (1968): 108–11. See Sarna, *Understanding Genesis,* 63–80.

"While the confounding of tongues came about," writes Kramer, "as the result of rivalry, . . . in the Sumerian case this was between god and god, and in the Hebrew, between god and man." Everything that can be tested in this eleventh chapter (e.g., the type of mortar and the type of architecture) leads us to conclude that the chapter has a genuine setting in Babylon.

V.   THE LITERARY STYLE

Now if subject matter, content, philological connections, and so-called impossibilities do not furnish us with either the rationale, the occasion, or the literary form (*Gattung*) for Genesis, will not the style and literary form of these units, when compared to the ancient Near Eastern epics, provide the key for identifying the type of literature?

W. F. Albright provided just such an example when he pointed to the "when . . . then . . ." translation for Genesis 1:1–3 as a definite borrowing of the Sumero-Babylonian style from the *Enuma Elish*.[52] Even this proposal, which makes the first two verses dependent statements with the main verb coming in verse 3, while being in and of itself based on a grammatical phenomenon, which can be illustrated elsewhere in the Hebrew Scriptures, the translation of a dependent clause does not meet all the demands of the text, as E. J. Young has pointed out.[53] Genesis 1:1 is an independent statement based on the following evidence: the disjunctive accent used by the Masoretes (thereby showing their early understanding), the ancient versions, the context, the position of the subject in verse 2, and the syntax of the three circumstantial clauses in verse 2 anticipating the main verb in verse 3. (See my discussion of this point in my chapter on Genesis 1).

---

[52] William F. Albright, "Review of Heidel, The Babylonian Genesis: The Story of Creation," Journal of Biblical Literature 62 (1943): 366–70.

[53] Edward J. Young, "The Relation of the First Two Verses of Genesis One to Verses Two and Three," *Westminster Theological Society* 21 (1959): 133–46. See also Young, "The Interpretation of Genesis 1:2," *Westminster Theological Society* 23 (1961): 151–78; cf. Heidel, *Babylonian Genesis*, 95. Also see Walther Eichrodt, "In the Beginning," in *Israel's Prophetic Heritage: Essays in Honor of James Muilenburg*, ed. B. W. Anderson and W. Harrelson (New York: Harper & Row, 1962), 1–10.

CONCLUSION

Based on all that has been presented here, we conclude that the suggested literary type (*Gattung*) of myth cannot be validated in content subject matter, individual words chosen, pre-scientific views of the world, style, or form. This is not to say that all modern scholars have chosen this form as the only possibility; but it does point out that almost all of the modern discussion borrows some or all of this form when it chooses to classify this section of Scripture. For example, Alan Richardson labels these chapters as "parables" because of the undesirable associations of our word "myth," but appeals to the same type of evidence we have been discussing in this appendix.

The writer's intention must be the first order of business if we are going to make any progress in locating the literary form for this section. We believe such an indicator is given to us by the recurring heading "these are the generations of."[54] In Genesis 12–50, the author uses this device five times to introduce each new patriarch, and in these chapters we have been experiencing a growing confirmation of the reliability of the record due to unprecedented archaeological finds relating to patriarchal customs, names, places, and times.[55] Is it not worth noting that the writer (or at least in the view of some—the editor[s]) also used this same device six times to introduce blocks of material in chapters 1–11?

The opening chapters of Genesis are just as vulnerable and just as exposed to the searching eye of the scholar in those tangible ways as

---

[54]   Genesis 2:4, 5:1, 6:9. 10:1, 11:10, 27, 25:12, 19, 36:1, (36:9), 37:2. Note also Numbers 3:1, Ruth 4:18, and Matthew 1:1. Malamat, "King Lists," 164–65, 170–71, compares the *toledot* of Perez (Ruth 4:18), for example, with the three *palus* ("eras," or "dynasties") of the Genealogy of the Hammurabi dynasty and guesses that the implication is that theme terms indicate earlier genealogical documents that were used as sources for the present compositions.

[55]   Recently there seems to be a growing undercurrent of rejecting the conclusion that the patriarchal names, customs, geography, and laws fit perfectly within the early second millennium as witnessed by such sites as Nuzu, Mari, and Alalakh. Illustrative of this point of view are Gene M. Tucker, "The Legal Background of Gen. 23," *Journal of Biblical Literature* 85 (1966): 77–84; and John Van Seters, "The Problem of Childlessness in New Eastern Law and the Patriarchs of Israel," *Journal of Biblical Literature* 87 (1968): 401–8; cf. a partial response of Kitchen, *Ancient Orient and the Old Testament*, 154–55.

Genesis 12–50. While the job is fantastically more difficult, the point is clear: there are sixty-four geographical terms; eighty-eight personal names; forty-eight generic names; and least twenty-one identifiable cultural items (such as gold, bdellium, onyx, brass, iron, gopher wood, bitumen, mortar, brick, stone, harp, pipe, cities, towers) in these opening chapters.[56] The significance of this list may be seen by comparing it, for example, with "the paucity of references in the Koran. Genesis 10 alone has five times more geographical data of importance than the whole of the Koran."[57] Every one of these items presents us with the possibility of establishing the reliability of our author.[58] The content runs head on into a description of the real world rather than recounting events belonging to another world level of reality.

Of course this does not exclude figures of speech and figurative language. E. W. Bullinger can list approximately 150 different items in these eleven chapters alone, illustrating one figure of speech or another.[59] The point is that this is all controlled objectively as a science. Further, to say something is a figure of speech is only to begin the problem; for we must say which figure it is, supply other examples as a comparative exegetical control, and then go on to assign a meaning that is in keeping with this figure of speech.

Neither are we left to our own devices when it comes to talking about such forms as poetry, parable, allegory, or apocalyptic-like literature. Each of these has its own control. Basically, there are two broad categories for arranging the material: poetry or prose. The decision is easy: Genesis 1–11 is prose and not poetry. The use of the *waw* consecutive with the verb to describe sequential acts, the frequent use of the direct object sign and the so-called relative pronoun, the stress on definitions, and the

[56] I am indebted to my assistant Arnold Conrad for supplying and documenting this list.

[57] Wilbur N. Smith, *Egypt in Prophecy* (Boston: Wilde, 1957), 13–23, especially 21–22n2.

[58] Some preliminary work has begun, for example, T. C. Mitchell, "Archaeology and Genesis i–xi," *Faith and Thought,* 91 (1959): 28–49. Also on Genesis 10: Donald J. Wiseman, "Genesis 10: Some Archaeological Considerations," *Journal of the Transactions of the Victorian Institute* 87 (1955): 14–24, 113–18.

[59] E. W. Bullinger, *Figures of Speech Used in the Bible* (1898; repr., Grand Rapids: Baker, 1968), 1032–33.

spreading out of these events in a sequential order indicates that we are in prose and not in poetry. Say what we will, the author plainly intends to be doing the same thing in these chapters that he is doing in chapters 12–50. If we want a sample of what the author's poetry, with its Hebrew parallelism and fixed pairs, would look like, Genesis 4:23–24 will serve as an illustration.[60]

Unfortunately, the verdict that we are dealing with prose is not the end of the discussion. Eissfeldt teaches us that there are three subgroups of prose forms: speeches, records, and narratives.[61]

While there seems to be very little to represent the subcategory of speeches, there are large sections in Genesis illustrating the second area called records. Included in this category are contracts, letters, lists, laws, and the two genealogical lists (5 and 11). It should be especially noted that Genesis 5:1 makes reference to a "letter" or "scroll" as a source for the list, which has the same formula that the writer uses elsewhere some ten times, that is, "the generations of." This could well indicate the author's free admission of his dependence upon sources and lists, just as the writers of the Old Testament historical books give us a veritable string of sources that they consulted as they moved from one historical period to another. Particularly instructive is the appearance of this identical formula at the end of the book of Ruth, which also gives us a list of ten generations and brings the reader down to the writer's own day, that is, the Davidic era. One should compare Luke's historical and literary methodology as he began to write his Gospel under the revelation and inspiration of the Triune God (Luke 1:1–4).

With large sections of the text of Genesis 1–11 still unmatched in form, we turn finally to the last subcategory of prose: narrative. But we are surprised to find two kinds of narrative prose: poetic narratives and prose narratives. Since the poetic narratives include myth, fairy tales, sagas, legends, anecdotes, and tales, the preceding discussion is all the more important. How shall we decide between historic and poetic narrative? The approach should be uniform for all biblical scholarship. But indeed let the hallmark of evangelical Old Testament research be the primacy of

---

[60] Mitchell, "Archaeology and Genesis i–xi," 48: "There is no plain indication that these chapters are couched in other than plain narrative prose."

[61] Otto Eissfeldt, *The Old Testament: An Introduction,* trans. Peter R. Ackroyd (New York: Harper & Row, 1965), 11ff.

the author's own truth intention, the full utilization of all tools of exegesis, and the constant reference to all the advantages available in the plethora of ancient Near Eastern materials. The difference in our results will mainly come in two areas: the alleged inviolability of the causal continuum of a space-time world in all instances, and the consistent restriction of mythological values to certain semantic terms on the part of some biblical scholars.

Happily, some have felt obliged to go beyond the acknowledged "Continental Divide" in biblical scholarship to show that these objections need not be so. Langdon B. Gilkey has written an article that must already be recognized as one of the greatest religious articles of our times.[62] He confesses that his stance and that of most modern scholarship is "half liberal and modern on the one hand, and half Biblical and orthodox on the other, i.e., its world view or cosmology is modern while its theological language is Biblical and orthodox."[63] He writes, "What has happened is clear: because of our modern cosmology, we have stripped what we regard as 'the Biblical point of view' of all its wonders and voices. . . . [W]e have rejected as invalid all the innumerable cases of God's acting and speaking."[64] We agree not only with Langdon's self-analysis but also with his solution; for he goes on to write, "First there is the job of stating what the Biblical writers meant to say, a statement couched in the Bible's own terms, cosmological, historical, and theological."[65]

Now the way back to the author's intention is through the words he uses. We believe along with J. Stafford Wright that the metaphorical use of words might relieve many of the semantic difficulties that we might otherwise instinctively class as mythological clues.[66] He illustrates our present heavy use of metaphors in such scientific terminology as used by psychoanalysis and analytical philosophy, for example, the subconscious, the superego, the depths of the psyche, the threshold of consciousness,

---

[62] Langdon B. Gilkey, "Cosmology, Ontology, and the Travail of Biblical Language," *Concordia Theological Monthly* 33 (1962): 143–54 (reprinted from *Journal of Religion,* 1961: 194–205).

[63] Ibid., 143.

[64] Ibid., 152.

[65] Ibid., 153.

[66] J. Stafford Wright, "The Place of Myth in the Interpretation of the Bible," *Journal of the Transactions of the Victorian Institute* 88 (1956): 18–30.

and so on. He warns, "A critical reader a thousand years hence might well think that the twentieth century held the idea of a three-story solid mind, with doors and gates. We know how wrong he would be; but we would still maintain that these phrases are legitimate metaphors, and indeed almost essential metaphors, to translate non-spatial and comprehensible language."[67] How shall we communicate spiritual realities into spatial terms? He even suggests that we ought to press behind the stories of such dragons as Tiamat, Leviathan, Lotan, and Rahab, which are common coin to the ancient Near Eastern writer and the Bible, "and ask whether the pagan religions may not themselves be preserving a primeval truth that underlies the biblical conception of the fall of Satan and the warfare between Satan and God."[68] At any rate, the proximity in time when these terms are used does not necessarily imply similarity in meaning for all the authors.

If we do not insist upon injecting these two a priori type of arguments into our exegesis, we believe the arguments illustrated above will yield the conclusion that we are dealing with the genre of historical narrative-prose, interspersed with some lists, sources, sayings, and poetic lines. The real key to the literary genus of this difficult section of Scripture is found in the author's recurring formula, "the generations of," which demonstrates his organization and his understanding of the materials.

---

[67] Ibid., 23.

[68] Ibid., 27.

NAME INDEX

SUBJECT INDEX

Scripture Index